# Organized Crime

CRIME, JUSTICE, AND PUNISHMENT

# Organized Crime

**Josh Wilker**

Austin Sarat, GENERAL EDITOR

CHELSEA HOUSE PUBLISHERS
Philadelphia

Frontis: *Murdered Mafia boss Carmine Galante, 1979.*

**Chelsea House Publishers**

*Editor in Chief* Stephen Reginald
*Managing Editor* James D. Gallagher
*Production Manager* Pamela Loos
*Art Director* Sara Davis
*Director of Photography* Judy L. Hasday
*Senior Production Editor* Lisa Chippendale

**Staff for ORGANIZED CRIME**

*Senior Editor* John Ziff
*Associate Art Director/Designer* Takeshi Takahashi
*Picture Researcher* Sandy Jones
*Cover Illustration* Takeshi Takahashi



First Printing

1 3 5 7 9 8 6 4 2

The Chelsea House World Wide Web site address is
**http://www.chelseahouse.com**

Library of Congress Cataloging-in-Publication Data

Wilker, Josh.
Organized crime / Josh Wilker; Austin Sarat, general editor.
p. 96. cm — (Crime, justice, and punishment)
Includes bibliographical references and index.
Summary: Recounts the history of organized crime from the Cosa Nostra to Al Capone to recent global criminal organizations.

ISBN 0-7910-4271-5 (hardcover)

1. Organized crime—United States—History—Juvenile literature.
[1. Organized crime.] I. Sarat, Austin. II. Title. III. Series.
HV6446.W53 1999
364.1'06'0973—dc21 98-47954
CIP
AC

# Contents

## Crime, Justice, and Punishment

Capital Punishment

Classic Cons and Swindles

The FBI's Most Wanted

Hate Crimes

Infamous Trials

The Jury System

Juvenile Crime

Organized Crime

Prisons

Private Investigators
and Bounty Hunters

Race, Crime, and Punishment

Revenge and Retribution

Rights of the Accused

Serial Murder

Terrorism

Victims and Victims' Rights

White-Collar Crime

# Fears and Fascinations:

## An Introduction to Crime, Justice, and Punishment

*By Austin Sarat*

We live with crime and images of crime all around us. Crime evokes in most of us a deep aversion, a feeling of profound vulnerability, but it also evokes an equally deep fascination. Today, in major American cities the fear of crime is a major fact of life, some would say a disproportionate response to the realities of crime. Yet the fear of crime is real, palpable in the quickened steps and furtive glances of people walking down darkened streets. At the same time, we eagerly follow crime stories on television and in movies. We watch with a "who done it" curiosity, eager to see the illicit deed done, the investigation undertaken, the miscreant brought to justice and given his just deserts. On the streets the presence of crime is a reminder of our own vulnerability and the precariousness of our taken-for-granted rights and freedoms. On television and in the movies the crime story gives us a chance to probe our own darker motives, to ask "Is there a criminal within?" as well as to feel the collective satisfaction of seeing justice done.

Fear and fascination, these two poles of our engagement with crime, are, of course, only part of the story. Crime is, after all, a major social and legal problem, not just an issue of our individual psychology. Politicians today use our fear of, and fascination with, crime for political advantage. How we respond to crime, as well as to the political uses of the crime issue, tells us a lot about who we are as a people as well as what we value and what we tolerate. Is our response compassionate or severe? Do we seek to understand or to punish, to enact an angry vengeance or to rehabilitate and welcome the criminal back into our midst? The CRIME, JUSTICE, AND PUNISHMENT series is designed to explore these themes, to ask why we are fearful and fascinated, to probe the meanings and motivations of crimes and criminals and of our responses to them, and, finally, to ask what we can learn about ourselves and the society in which we live by examining our responses to crime.

Crime is always a challenge to the prevailing normative order and a test of the values and commitments of law-abiding people. It is sometimes a Raskolnikov-like act of defiance, an assertion of the unwillingness of some to live according to the rules of conduct laid out by organized society. In this sense, crime marks the limits of the law and reminds us of law's all-too-regular failures. Yet sometimes there is more desperation than defiance in criminal acts; sometimes they signal a deep pathology or need in the criminal. To confront crime is thus also to come face-to-face with the reality of social difference, of class privilege and extreme deprivation, of race and racism, of children neglected, abandoned, or abused whose response is to enact on others what they have experienced themselves. And occasionally crime, or what is labeled a criminal act, represents a call for justice, an appeal to a higher moral order against the inadequacies of existing law.

Figuring out the meaning of crime and the motivations of criminals and whether crime arises from defiance, desperation, or the appeal for justice is never an easy task. The motivations and meanings of crime are as varied as are the persons who engage in criminal conduct. They are as mysterious as any of the mysteries of the human soul. Yet the desire to know the secrets of crime and the criminal is a strong one, for in that knowledge may lie one step on the road to protection, if not an assurance of one's own personal safety. Nonetheless, as strong as that desire may be, there is no available technology that can allow us to know the whys of crime with much confidence, let alone a scientific certainty. We can, however, capture something about crime by studying the defiance, desperation, and quest for justice that may be associated with it. Books in the CRIME, JUSTICE, AND PUNISHMENT series will take up that challenge. They tell stories of crime and criminals, some famous, most not, some glamorous and exciting, most mundane and commonplace.

This series will, in addition, take a sober look at American criminal justice, at the procedures through which we investigate crimes and identify criminals, at the institutions in which innocence or guilt is determined. In these procedures and institutions we confront the thrill of the chase as well as the challenge of protecting the rights of those who defy our laws. It is through the efficiency and dedication of law enforcement that we might capture the criminal; it is in the rare instances of their corruption or brutality that we feel perhaps our deepest betrayal. Police, prosecutors, defense lawyers, judges, and jurors administer criminal justice and in their daily actions give substance to the guarantees of the Bill of Rights. What is an adversarial system of justice? How does it work? Why do we have it? Books in the CRIME, JUSTICE, AND PUNISHMENT series will examine the thrill of the chase as we seek to capture the criminal. They will also reveal the drama and majesty of the criminal trial as well as the day-to-day reality of a criminal justice system in which trials are the exception and negotiated pleas of guilty are the rule.

When the trial is over or the plea has been entered, when we have separated the innocent from the guilty, the moment of punishment has arrived. The injunction to punish the guilty, to respond to pain inflicted by inflicting pain, is as old as civilization itself. "An eye for an eye and a tooth for a tooth" is a biblical reminder that punishment must measure pain for pain. But our response to the criminal must be better than and different from the crime itself. The biblical admonition, along with the constitutional prohibition of "cruel and unusual punishment," signals that we seek to punish justly and to be just not only in the determination of who can and should be punished, but in how we punish as well. But neither reminder tells us what to do with the wrongdoer. Do we rape the rapist, or burn the home of the arsonist? Surely justice and decency say no. But, if not, then how can and should we punish? In a world in which punishment is neither identical to the crime nor an automatic response to it, choices must be made and we must make them. Books in the CRIME, JUSTICE, AND PUNISHMENT series will examine those choices and the practices, and politics, of punishment. How do we punish and why do we punish as we do? What can we learn about the rationality and appropriateness of today's responses to crime by examining our past and its responses? What works? Is there, and can there be, a just measure of pain?

CRIME, JUSTICE, AND PUNISHMENT brings together books on some of the great themes of human social life. The books in this series capture our fear and fascination with crime and examine our responses to it. They remind us of the deadly seriousness of these subjects. They bring together themes in law, literature, and popular culture to challenge us to think again, to think anew, about subjects that go to the heart of who we are and how we can and will live together.

* * * * *

Several things seem unalterably true about organized crime. First, as the name indicates, it is neither random nor merely deviant, but instead reflects an alternative social formation in which criminal activity is central. Organized crime is indeed highly organized and normatively driven. Whether in gangs or more elaborate social forms, organized crime has its own rules and hierarchies, including a kind of alternative legal system. Second, this alternative legal system sanctions a high level of violence, which often leads to an escalating cycle of bloodshed and retaliation. Third, organized crime has often been well integrated into certain ethnic groups and has provided one vehicle through which members of those groups have gained power and position within American society.

And yet, the forms and functions of organized crime are not the same today as they were a century ago. Different ethnic groups have become more prominent in organized criminal activities, and those activities have gone global. We need to think about this kind of crime as a genuinely international phenomenon, with roots and connections in many different nations. Finally, the challenges of fighting and responding to organized crime are very different from those faced by law enforcement in dealing with other types of crime. Measuring success in this area is difficult, since the phenomenon itself is virtually invisible.

This book presents a vivid and compelling portrait of a phenomenon that is as difficult to understand as it is important. Drawing on case histories, documentary sources, and a keen attentiveness to the forms and meanings of organized criminal activity, it gives us a no-holds-barred account of the inner workings of organized crime as well as its place in American society. As readable as it is rooted in rigorous research, *Organized Crime* will leave few readers unmoved, and few will come away without a deep and rich understanding of the challenges organized crime poses for our society.

# The Dust of Life

In 1983, an 11-year-old boy named Tinh Ngo was sent away from home by his parents in Vietnam. The boy didn't want to leave, but his parents saw no future for their son in the war-torn, impoverished country. From beautiful photographs of mansions and natural vistas sent to them by a family friend in California, they got the idea that Tinh could find a better life in America.

*Dream-turned-nightmare: Like these Vietnamese "boat people," Tinh Ngo left his troubled homeland as a boy in search of a better life. His search led him to the streets of New York City and membership in a deadly Vietnamese gang called Born to Kill.*

A trip to a refugee camp in Malaysia aboard a small, rickety boat packed with 30 other refugees was supposed to take three days, but it dragged on longer after the boat drifted off course. Two pirate ships raided the boat, robbing and violently menacing Tinh and the other passengers. After 12 days, the boat drifted aimlessly, out of fuel, with buzzards circling overhead. Tinh and the other passengers were saved by a passing Panamanian oil tanker that happened to catch sight of them. After the rescue, Tinh spent nearly two years at a crowded, filthy refugee camp in southern Thailand.

In late 1985, Tinh was allowed to board a plane to America. The golden future his parents had envisioned was nowhere to be seen, however. Over the next four years, Tinh lived in a succession of poor, crime-ridden neighborhoods, housed by various foster parents who were less interested in Tinh's welfare than in the money they received from the government for taking him in. One of Tinh's foster brothers sold crack cocaine out of their foster home. At school, Tinh was routinely ridiculed for his heavy accent by American-born kids, who called him "slant eyes" and "gook." It seemed to him that if this was the promised land, he didn't belong.

The first time he ever got the feeling that he wasn't totally alone in his new world was when he started frequenting a pool hall in his New York City neighborhood. It was there that a group of teenagers who were also from Vietnam hung out. They had backgrounds similar to Tinh Ngo's, many of them also sent out into the world alone by their parents in hopes that they would find a better life in America. Older, more well-established Vietnamese immigrants had a name for the newer arrivals like Tinh Ngo and the others at the pool hall. They called them *bui dui*, a Vietnamese phrase meaning "the dust of life."

But to Tinh, finding the pool hall was like finding a safe haven during a storm. Everywhere he had been since coming to the United States, he had gotten the feeling that he wasn't wanted. The guys who hung out at the pool hall didn't make him feel that way. They made him feel that he belonged.

They were part of a violent Vietnamese street gang called Born to Kill.

● ● ●

By drifting into the middle of the Born to Kill gang, Tinh Ngo unknowingly became part of the multi-billion-dollar business known as organized crime. Analyst James Cook estimated in 1982 that organized crime in the United States generated $150 billion a year in revenue. Four years later, experts at Fishman and Wharton Econometric Forecasting Associates came up with the smaller (but still mind-boggling) figure of $46 billion a year. The Fishman and Wharton researchers and analysts also estimated that criminal organizations employed 281,487 people directly while producing another half a million related jobs.

For many years, the public perception was that the term *organized crime* was simply another way of referring to the Italian crime group known as the Mafia. In fact, the Mafia is only one among a sprawling collection of crime groups that make up the organized crime industry. Many of these groups are large, highly systematized, and efficient conglomerates, run with the kind of methodical planning and job specialization that is seen in multinational corporations.

By definition, organized crime must involve action by a group, which distinguishes it from the multitude of crimes committed by individuals. It must be motivated solely by the desire for money, distinguishing it from, for example, a bias-motivated hate crime or a politically motivated act of terrorism. Organized crime must also be an ongoing activity rather than an isolated act. But even when a group motivated solely by a desire for money commits a series of crimes—for example, a string of bank robberies—that group isn't necessarily an organized crime group.

All organized crime groups, large and small, must have a well-established hierarchy of power. Born to Kill, for example, was ruled over by a Vietnamese immigrant named David Thai; gang enforcer Lan Ngoc Tran served as the gang's second-in-command; and other members known as *Dai Los* (a term meaning "big brother") oversaw the gang's day-to-day activities in the various areas where the gang had established a presence.

The various groups involved in organized crime also

share the desire to make money in a wide variety of illicit ways. Among the ever-growing list of profit-producing crimes these organizations engage in are extortion, illegal gambling, loan-sharking, robbery, tax scams, kidnapping, counterfeiting, prostitution, the smuggling of illegal aliens, and the smuggling and sale of illegal drugs such as marijuana, heroin, and cocaine.

All organized crime groups also share the complete willingness to fuel their illicit business endeavors with violence or the threat of violence. Simply put, in organized crime, violence or the threat of violence increases the flow of money into the hands of the criminals. Tinh Ngo saw this principle at work while accompanying members of the Born to Kill gang on visits to Vietnamese-owned stores to demand what is known as "lucky money." With very few exceptions, the store owners paid, fearing violent retaliation if they did not. A store owner named Sen Van Ta, after choosing not to pay, was shot to death in broad daylight by Born to Kill enforcer Lan Ngoc Tran.

Violence or the threat of violence also intimidates (or even eliminates) would-be competitors. It promotes discipline and secrecy within the organization. It tends to silence citizens who might otherwise be tempted to testify in court against the organized lawbreakers. Also, in many cases, organized crime groups have shown a willingness to use violence against judges, politicians, journalists, and law enforcement professionals attempting to combat their activities. In the late 1980s and early 1990s in Colombia, for example, well over a thousand public officials (including four presidential candidates), police officers, and journalists were murdered by Colombian drug cartels.

Methodical killing sprees like the ones ordered by the leaders of the Colombian cartels make it easy to see why some experts on the subject of organized crime, like U.S. senator John Kerry, refer to the battle between organized crime and the forces opposed to it as a war.

*Eight officers died and 10 were wounded when a truck bomb exploded outside this Bogotá police station. Corruption, intimidation, and murder helped Colombian drug cartels subvert the institutions of their country.*

Historically, the foot soldiers who engage in this war on the side of organized crime have often been impoverished urban youths who see little hope of finding a legitimate place in their society. They have often been, in other words, very much like Tinh Ngo.

❦ ❦ ❦

As Tinh Ngo participated in various illegal activities with the Born to Kill gang, he found himself resisting the kind of violent acts that create the climate of fear organized crime thrives in. Other gang members, especially Lan Ngoc Tran, had no such reservations. Tran had grown up during the bloodiest years of the war in his country and had learned how to kill at an age when most American kids are learning how to drive. Gary Palmer, an investigator into Vietnamese gang activity who had formerly worked as a Marine interrogator in Vietnam, described the frightening origins of Vietnamese gang leaders like Lan Tran, saying, "They're the guys who floated up rivers in North Vietnam to assassinate people. To blow away a guy is nothing to them."

Tinh Ngo saw with his own eyes what Lan Tran was capable of when, during a bungled robbery attempt by the gang in Georgia, the enforcer coldly shot store owner Odum Lim in the head. Lim managed to survive, but Tinh didn't know this as the scene replayed itself in his mind again and again in the months following the robbery. As he struggled through a string of sleepless nights, he kept seeing Lan Tran's emotionless eyes, hearing the thunderous sound of the gun, and then seeing Lim lying in a pool of blood on the floor. It kept occurring to Tinh that the man who'd been shot had done nothing wrong.

At the time Odum Lim was shot, an investigation into the Born to Kill gang was under way in New York City, headed by agent Dan Kumor of the Bureau of Alcohol, Tobacco, and Firearms. All Kumor knew about Born to Kill when he'd started the investigation was what he'd read in the newspapers: they were the gang that, while burying a slain comrade, had gotten attacked in a cemetery by a rival gang armed with automatic weapons. At first, this frightening kernel of information was only supplemented by additional evidence that a shockingly high level of violence—even by the standards of organized crime—seemed to follow the Born to Kill gang wherever it went. Kumor and his fellow investigators couldn't find the kind of evidence that would bring the gang down. Then Tinh Ngo was arrested for a robbery he'd been involved in before the robbery in Georgia.

Even before the shooting of Odum Lim, Tinh had been thinking about leaving the gang. The initial sense of belonging he had gotten from joining the gang had become increasingly overshadowed by a feeling that life

*As longtime chairman of the U.S. Senate Subcommittee on Terrorism, Narcotics, and International Operations, John Kerry of Massachusetts became an expert on organized crime. In their reach and scope, he believes, today's criminal organizations "make the gangs of the past look like mom-and-pop operations."*

in the gang was nothing more than an endless cycle of violence. He knew it wouldn't be easy to leave the gang, which didn't look kindly on deserters. Furthermore, Tinh Ngo didn't know any life beyond the gang. But the Odum Lim shooting pushed Tinh Ngo past his fears of leaving the gang. When he was arrested, he began to talk. What most amazed the investigators about Tinh Ngo's cooperation was that he never once asked them what was in it for him. He seemed to want to tell them all he knew about the gang, as if he was trying to clear his conscience.

In the difficult fight against organized crime, insider information is one of the few reliable tools that investigators can use. Without insiders, investigators are in the dark. Another tool used increasingly by investigators is the covert recording of conversations of suspected gang members. Often these recordings serve as the best way of tying the leaders of a crime group to the various crimes that are committed upon their orders. At the urging of the investigators, Tinh Ngo started wearing a recording device whenever he met with Lan Tran or David Thai.

Tinh Ngo began tipping the investigators off to crimes the gang had planned, and the investigators were able to step in and prevent them from happening. Often, to protect the investigation (and Tinh Ngo), Kumor and his staff had to come up with ingenious ways to disguise the fact that they had gotten inside information. The closest call came after Tinh alerted them that two Born to Kill members were on their way to bomb a restaurant in Chinatown. Investigators believe that the bombing was to be in retaliation for disparaging remarks about the gang uttered in the press by the restaurant owner.

Kumor, with no more than seconds to spare, was able to apprehend the two bomb-carrying gang members a few feet away from the crowded restaurant. Soon investigators, with tremendous help from Tinh Ngo's inside information, were able to defuse the Born to Kill gang, arresting its members and prosecuting them under the Racketeer Influenced and Corrupt Organizations (RICO) laws, which have proven to be the most effective prosecution tool yet devised in combating organized crime. Born to Kill was taken off the streets of New York City.

Born to Kill was brought down by a variety of factors. One of these factors was that a gang member, prompted by moral revulsion at his associates' violent behavior, began working against the gang from the inside. Another factor was that a team of investigators, including federal agents and city police detectives, worked tirelessly on the case. But the third, and perhaps most important, factor in the gang's demise was that it had not been around long enough to establish the kind of deep roots and financial stability that other organized crime groups have established.

Other, more deeply rooted, crime groups persist. Senator Kerry, in his book *The New War,* about the international web of crime now imperiling America, observed that the more streamlined and advanced crime groups currently in action "make the gangs of the past look like mom-and-pop operations." As a new century approaches, sophisticated crime groups from China, Colombia, Cuba, Italy, and Russia all seem to have laid down deep roots in American soil.

If these roots are ever to be pulled out, Americans must first gain an understanding of the history of organized crime in the United States, a history that began in the 19th century, in ragged gangs that formed in run-down, rat-infested urban neighborhoods. It began with castaway street kids not unlike Tinh Ngo. It began in the dust of life.

2.

# An Alternate Route to the American Dream

"Debauchery has made the very houses prematurely old," wrote Charles Dickens in the middle of the 19th century, describing the area of Manhattan's Lower East Side known as the Five Points. "See how the rotten beams are tumbling down, and how the patched and broken windows seem to scowl dimly, like eyes that have been hurt in drunken frays. . . . [A]ll that is loathsome, drooping and decayed is here."

The Five Points, so named because of the intersection of five streets near what is today Foley Square, proved to be fertile ground for the development of organized crime in America. A large, overcrowded immigrant population inhabited the neighborhood. These newcomers had to endure great hardships from the moment they arrived in America, often starting out with little or no money, facing the difficulties of learning a new language and a new culture, and suffering from widespread discrimination against them by poten-

*New York City's Lower East Side, 1889. From crowded, poverty-stricken immigrant neighborhoods such as this one emerged the street gangs that would eventually evolve into organized crime groups.*

*William Marcy "Boss" Tweed, head of the Tammany Hall political organization. Tweed elevated government corruption to an art form in 19th-century New York.*

tial employers. The great majority of the immigrants found legitimate ways to overcome the difficult situation they were thrust into upon reaching America. But some of them, finding the doors to legitimate work difficult to open, began doing illegitimate work.

In their book *Organized Crime in America,* Dennis Kenney and James Finckenauer write, "Those with little formal education and few economic resources find that they are denied the opportunity to acquire money and other success symbols legally. One response is criminal solutions. A cardinal American virtue, ambition, promotes a cardinal American vice, deviant behavior. Crime in general, and organized crime in particular, is simply an alternate route to the American dream."

The movement toward widespread organized crime in America began when youths started banding together into street gangs for self-protection and to strengthen their own sense of identity. The gangs were spontaneous creations, not formed with the idea that they would become criminal organizations. However, a progression toward criminal endeavors was set in motion by the formation of the gangs.

One of the earlier evidences of crimes being committed by gangs of the Five Points was not sophisticated at all. The gang known as the Whyos circulated a menu advertising its services:

Punching . . . . . . . . . . . . . . . . . . . . . . . . . . . . $2
Both eyes blacked. . . . . . . . . . . . . . . . . . . . . . . $4
Nose and jaw broke . . . . . . . . . . . . . . . . . . $10
Jacked out [knocked out with a blackjack] . . . $15
Ear chawed off . . . . . . . . . . . . . . . . . . . . . . $15
Leg or arm broke. . . . . . . . . . . . . . . . . . . . . $19
Shot in leg . . . . . . . . . . . . . . . . . . . . . . . . . $25
Stab . . . . . . . . . . . . . . . . . . . . . . . . . . . . . . $25
Doing the big job . . . . . . . . . . . . . $100 and up

In the biggest American metropolises of the middle to late 1800s, New York City and Chicago, the brutal yet simplistic activities of the gangs gradually became intertwined with two more-organized entities, politics and gambling. Proprietors of gambling houses used the gangs to protect their establishments. Politicians used the gangs to strong-arm voters into stuffing the ballot boxes in their favor.

Big Mike McDonald ran the city of Chicago from his saloon and gambling casino, exerting influence on every level of the city government, from low-ranking police officers to the mayor. The apex of McDonald's reign came during the 1893 World's Fair in Chicago, where small-time criminals like pickpockets, muggers, and con men were assigned specific streets throughout the city on which to work their nefarious crafts. McDonald skimmed from the earnings of all these criminals while using his political influence to make sure that no police action would interrupt any of their various endeavors.

In the late 1800s in New York City, politics and crime went hand in hand, as presided over by William Marcy "Boss" Tweed. Tweed, the leader of the Tammany Hall political organization that dominated city politics at that time, used the gangs to bully voters. Once in power, Tweed's men went about defrauding taxpayers with an endless parade of bogus construction projects. The intertwining of gambling, politics, and street-level violence in Tweed's city was symbolized by the rise to power of an ex-convict named John Morrissey. Morrissey, a former professional boxer, first came to the attention of a gambler with powerful political connections known as Captain Isaiah Rynders by venturing into Rynders's saloon and challenging everyone inside to a fight. The patrons of the bar complied, and Morrissey was eventually beaten, but not before dealing out considerable damage to his foes. The duly impressed Rynders began using Morrissey as an enforcer. Morrissey's penchant for brutality helped him gain widespread connections in the thoroughly corrupt Tammany city government. He parlayed these connections into a position as a powerful gambling hall owner with influence over gambling rackets all over the city. The ex-convict capped his meteoric rise by getting himself elected to Congress in 1866.

By the turn of the century, the gangs were becoming more organized. In fact, in New York City, two gangs in particular met virtually every defining characteristic of an organized crime group. These characteristics are: 1) that the group engage in a diversity of crimes; 2) that they show a propensity for violence; 3) that they are motivated by nothing more than a desire for profit; 4) that the group has a hierarchy with a boss at the top of it; 5) that the crimes they commit are planned out (that is, there is a criminal conspiracy involved in their execution); and 6) that the group is self-perpetuating (in other words, it survives from one generation to the next).

Only the last of these, that the group be self-perpetuating, fails to characterize the two gangs that ruled the Lower East Side of Manhattan at the turn of the century. These two gangs, Monk Eastman's Eastmans and Paul Kelly's Five Pointers, delved into gambling, extortion, robbery, and prostitution. But when the two gang leaders moved on, one to jail and the other to a wealthy semiretirement, the gangs found themselves

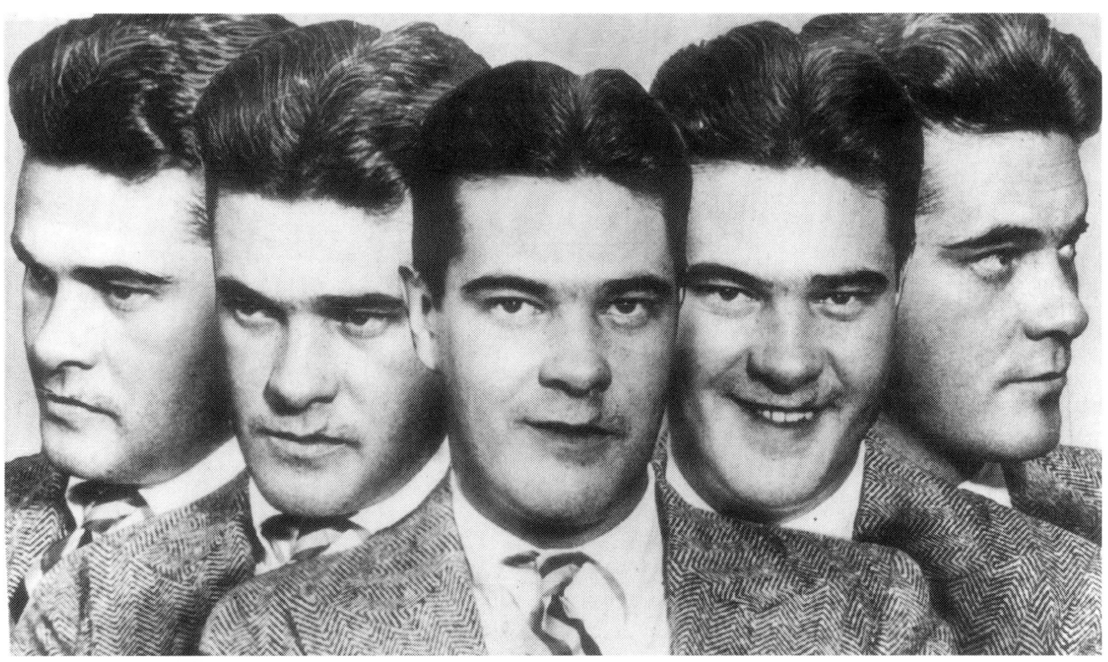

*Paul Kelly, head of the Five Points Gang, mugs for the camera in this multiple-exposure photo. Kelly and Monk Eastman, head of the rival Eastmans Gang, presided over criminal organizations that displayed all the characteristics of organized crime groups save one: their gangs weren't self-perpetuating. When Kelly and Eastman moved on, the Five Pointers and the Eastmans withered away.*

unable to continue. Organized crime in America had not yet reached the self-perpetuating stage.

This stage was on its way in Chicago and New York as the 1920s neared. It was then that organized crime would receive a jump-start: Congress would pass Prohibition, the ill-fated attempt to rid the United States of alcohol. But before Prohibition came about, two criminally inclined organizers were planting the seeds for the criminal syndicates of the future in Chicago and New York.

In Chicago the man was Mont Tennes, a gambler who knew how to capitalize on changing technology. He used intimidation tactics to grab hold of a monopoly in the telegraph business, which allowed him to capture a gambling monopoly as well, since at that time horse-racing results were reported over telegraph lines. Any gambling hall hoping to make money in the lucrative horse-race betting racket had to do so with the blessing of Mont Tennes.

At the same time Tennes was centralizing criminal

rackets in Chicago, New York City–based Arnold Rothstein was setting down a blueprint for his various corrupt pursuits that organized crime leaders would follow for decades to come. Rothstein didn't have the same background as most of the gangsters of his time. He came from the upper middle class rather than from a poor immigrant family. His father, who made a substantial living in the dry-goods business, often settled community squabbles and was known for his sense of ethics and fairness as "Abe the Just." What drew Rothstein into crime was a particular addiction that he developed early in life. "I didn't go to school much," Rothstein said. "But I used to gamble a lot and lose."

After learning the crooked lay of the land in the city under Big Tim Sullivan, a corrupt politician and gambler who had taken a liking to him, Rothstein went into business for himself, opening a gambling house on 46th Street. The location was notable in that it was the first time an establishment of its kind had been opened in a part of the city where gang activity wasn't particularly high. Rothstein clearly had designs on a criminal empire beyond the boundaries laid down by gang leaders of the past like Monk Eastman and Paul Kelly.

Rothstein became known as "the Brain," a nickname that aptly described his position as a kind of central intelligence for all criminal activity in the city. Rothstein funded and oversaw gambling rackets and drug-smuggling rings; he supplied thugs to industry leaders to break labor strikes while also occasionally renting out gang toughs to the unions, thus making money on both sides of labor disputes; and, during Prohibition, he got a piece of every kind of action available in the illegal liquor business.

Some gangsters in the city resented Rothstein's ubiquitous presence. "The mobsters hated him," recalled a Broadway financier of the time named Nils Granlund, "but because he had cash to loan when they needed it, they had to go to him. He had something to do with every speakeasy [illegal bar], he financed rumrunners and the hijackers who [stole from the rumrunners]."

On the other hand, the gangsters who saw that they could learn from Rothstein seemed to think quite highly of him. Meyer Lansky, who would go on after his informal apprenticeship under Rothstein to help build a nationwide organized crime empire, said, "Rothstein had the most remarkable brain. We all admired him. He was always totally honest with us and taught us a great deal. We got on well right from the beginning—like me he was a gambler from the cradle."

Rothstein's gambling habit eventually proved his undoing: he was shot to death in 1928, apparently for his failure to make good on a $316,000 poker debt. At the time of his death, police seized papers in his possession that proved his significant connections to politicians and gangsters alike. The papers also contained information on a multimillion-dollar drug-smuggling ring and tied him inextricably to the infamous fixing of the 1919 World Series.

Rothstein's legacy was the wide-ranging and organized way he oversaw the various rackets he was involved in. He trained a host of young gangsters who would go on to form a veritable who's who of organized crime: Lansky, Bugsy Siegel, Lucky Luciano, Dutch Schultz, Frank Costello, Waxey Gordon, Legs Diamond. These gangsters, along with a Chicago-based crime boss named Johnny Torrio, and Torrio's bombastic enforcer, Al Capone, would begin their rise to power shortly after the addition to the U.S. Constitution of the Eighteenth Amendment, which outlawed the manufacture, sale, import, or export of alcoholic beverages.

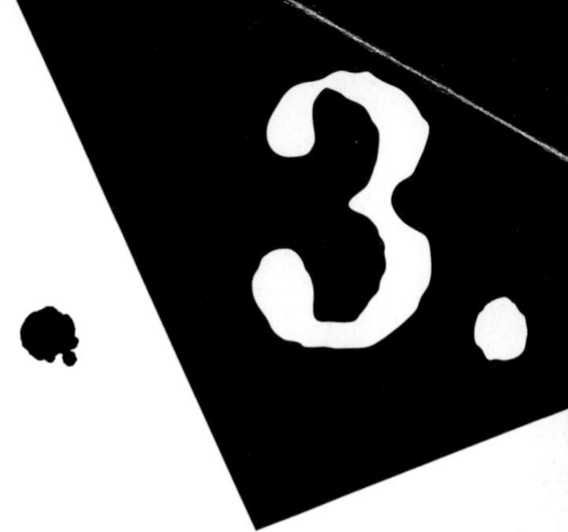

# "The Profits Were Tremendous"

In the early years of his life in crime, Irving Wexler eked out a living as a pickpocket on the Lower East Side. He might have remained a small-time criminal for his entire life if not for the passage of the Eighteenth Amendment. Within a few years after the beginning of Prohibition, Waxey Gordon, as Wexler came to be known, was pulling in profits of one to two million dollars a year. He ran his personal business interests like a corporation, operating out of a luxurious suite of offices in midtown Manhattan. He controlled portions of virtually every facet of the illegal liquor trade, from breweries and distilleries to nightclubs and the illegal bars known as speakeasies. He purchased a fleet of expensive cars so he could cut an impressive figure while being chauffeured around town, and the extravagant castle he called home was surrounded by a genuine King Arthur–style moat.

*Dumping a truckload of contraband beer, 1924. More than any other single factor, Prohibition, the ill-fated attempt to rid the United States of alcohol, spurred the development of organized crime.*

Waxey Gordon was far from being the only common street hood to hit it big during Prohibition. The bonanza of illegal opportunities created by the ban on alcohol made millionaires out of gangsters across the nation. More significantly, the demands of the highly profitable illegal alcohol trade spurred these gangsters on to form alliances and to increase the level of organization in their various criminal pursuits. In 13 years, from 1920 until the ratification in 1933 of the Twenty-first Amendment, which ended Prohibition, organized crime in America came of age, growing from a loose collection of unaffiliated gangs into a brutally efficient and wildly successful national industry.

Prohibition had come about in large part because of the strong political influence of a group called the Anti-Saloon League, which championed the opinion that alcohol was an evil substance leading America to ruin. The Anti-Saloon League and its many supporters, in a perpetual state of feverish moral outrage, neglected to consider fully the practical consequences of the constitutional amendment they prodded Congress into passing. They didn't foresee that the demand for alcohol would remain high. They didn't foresee that organizations operating outside the law would emerge to capitalize on the continuing demand for alcohol. And most of all, they didn't foresee that the new law would prove virtually impossible to enforce, efforts to do so often seeming like those of a man trying to halt a rushing river with his bare hands.

While the supporters of Prohibition optimistically envisioned a future in which all of America would be free of alcohol, gangsters across the country began working to bring about a different kind of future. It didn't take long for this alternative future to start taking shape. On January 15, 1920, the day before Prohibition was officially set to begin, $100,000 worth of whiskey was stolen from a government warehouse in Chicago.

The warehouse heist belonged to the more chaotic early attempts to circumvent the new law. In the two biggest cities in America, these disorganized efforts soon developed into a more systematic approach to the new illegal business. In both cities, this new method was largely orchestrated by two different men who had earned the nickname "the Brain": Arnold Rothstein and Johnny Torrio.

In New York City, Rothstein came up with the idea (and the money to back it) of establishing an operation that came to be known as "Rum Row." Ships full of whiskey from England would drop anchor three miles from the American shore, thus remaining in international waters and out of the jurisdiction of U.S. law enforcement. Speedboats were then dispatched to race portions of the liquor shipment back to the shore. Rothstein ensured that the operation ran smoothly by paying Coast Guard officials and local police to look the other way. In some cases, members of the Coast Guard even pitched in, helping to load the cases of liquor from the speedboats onto trucks headed for the city.

The degree of corruption in law enforcement during Prohibition started off at a high level and rose steadily. The Prohibition Bureau, set up specifically to enforce the new law, quickly distinguished itself as the most thoroughly crooked wing of law enforcement, its low-paid agents often proving to be easily bought by wealthy criminals like Rothstein. The general lack of resistance from lawmen, coupled with the high public demand for alcohol, allowed the bootlegging business to thrive.

"I thought it was too good to be true," said a mobster named Joe Bonanno, looking back on the era that, as with so many other mobsters, started his life in crime on a high note. "It seemed fairly safe in that the police didn't bother you. There was plenty of business for everyone. The profits were tremendous. And let's face it, especially for a young man, it was a lot of fun."

No one had as much fun with Prohibition in the beginning as Arnold Rothstein. While Rothstein skimmed money off the top of a myriad of different Prohibition operations, he served as a mentor to a host of young and ambitious gangsters. Some of these budding mobsters, like Waxey Gordon, Legs Diamond, and Dutch Schultz, got rich quick and reveled in the notoriety that their extravagant wealth brought. All three of them were dead or penniless within a few years of the start of their meteoric rise. Rothstein's more astute pupils heeded his advice to strive for high levels of organization in their rackets while keeping a low personal profile. Three men in particular, Lucky Luciano, Frank Costello, and Meyer Lansky, developed Rothstein's ideas into concrete plans that would shape organized crime in America for decades to come.

In 1927, Costello, Luciano, and Lansky spearheaded the formation of an unprecedented partnership between the major East Coast gangs. The partnership, known initially as the Big Seven Group, rapidly expanded to include at least 22 gangs, creating a web of organized crime that stretched from the northeastern cities of Boston and New York City south to Florida and west beyond the Mississippi River. The swelling power of the group enticed Chicago crime lord Johnny Torrio to emerge from his recent semiretirement. With the addition of Torrio's power and influence to the Big Seven Group, organized crime was on its way to becoming a nationwide syndicate.

Torrio, like many of the gangsters who got rich during Prohibition, had spent his teenage years in a gang on the Lower East Side. His innate penchant for viciousness earned him the nickname "Terrible Johnny" during his time as a member of Paul Kelly's Five Points Gang. This willingness to do violence would serve Torrio well throughout his career, as would his ability to learn from Paul Kelly, his suave, organized, and forward-looking gang boss. By the time Torrio was summoned to Chicago by a distant relative, mob boss James Colosimo, he had grown into the perfect agent of organized crime: he was reserved, efficient, and ready to kill. Unfortunately for Colosimo, Terrible Johnny was also

*Though he cultivated a public image as a philanthropist, Chicago crime boss Al Capone was a ruthless killer.*

opportunistic and enormously ambitious.

Torrio was initially brought to Chicago in 1909 to deal with a group called the Black Hand, which was trying to extort money from Colosimo. After solving his boss's problem by orchestrating the murder of several members of the extortion group, Torrio rose quickly in Colosimo's organization, which was chiefly a prostitution racket. With the passage of the Eighteenth Amendment in 1919, Torrio saw that the organization could grow by leaps and bounds by getting into the illegal liquor trade. Colosimo, already a wealthy man, saw no reason to expand his operation. Five months after the beginning of Prohibition, Colosimo was gunned down in the vestibule of his café—according to some accounts by Frankie Yale, a hired killer from New York City with close connections to Torrio.

With the reluctant Colosimo out of the way, Torrio dove into the business of smuggling and selling illegal liquor. He got a leg up on his many competitors by moving his operation out beyond Chicago city limits, to the suburban town of Cicero. In Chicago, law enforcement agents had made it somewhat difficult (though far from impossible) to do business by raiding speakeasies and warehouses. Many corrupt agents also cut into the profits of the burgeoning racket by constantly demanding hefty bribes in exchange for the promise to let illegal activities go unreported. By moving out of Chicago, Torrio eluded these hindrances while remaining close to the abundance of customers in the city.

Torrio, sensing the possibility of gaining complete control over the politicians and law enforcement officers in the small town, envisioned Cicero as an unassailable haven for his operation. He brought this vision to pass by force, setting loose his brutal right-hand man on the town. Cicero became a true sanctuary of crime soon after Al Capone arrived there.

Capone had fled to Chicago in 1919 after shooting a man in a barroom melee in New York City. Though he had not distinguished himself in any way in the criminal rackets in New York City, he quickly earned a place high in Torrio's gang, mainly by virtue of his volcanic temper. In Cicero, he displayed this quality in abundance. Once, Capone kicked the town's mayor down the steps of the courthouse as a cowed policeman walked by, doing nothing. On another occasion, a trustee defying Torrio and Capone was dragged out of a town council meeting and pummeled senseless on the street with a clublike weapon called a blackjack.

With his own business booming, Torrio sought to unify the various gangs of Chicago into one cooperative organization (which he planned to preside over, of course). One testament to Torrio's growing power was that by the middle of the 1920s he had pressured Mont Tennes, once the most powerful gangster in Chicago, into becoming a submissive member of Torrio's own organization. Tennes rightly saw that his only choices in the matter were to do what Torrio suggested, get out of the business altogether, or die.

One gang leader who double-crossed Torrio and Capone in 1924, Dion O'Bannion, ended up a corpse riddled with bullets in the flower shop that served as a front for his operation. O'Bannion's powerful gang retaliated, sparking a bloody underworld war that raged for five years. The increased level of violence in Chicago eventually proved to be too much for the man who helped bring it about. Johnny Torrio, after being critically wounded by O'Bannion gunmen in 1925, decided to retire, leaving his operation in the murderous hands of Capone.

Capone pushed forward Torrio's plan to monopolize the Chicago liquor business with all the finesse of a charging rhino. Unlike most mob bosses, who shy away from committing violent acts once they have risen to the top of their organizations, Capone often seemed to relish the chance to personally engage in lethal mayhem. In one exemplary incident, Capone punished two unfaithful members of his gang by beating them to death with a baseball bat. He also turned up the heat in his war with the rival O'Bannion gang, which in turn quickly made him their primary target. On one occasion, members of the O'Bannion gang emptied a thousand rounds of machine-gun ammunition into Capone's headquarters in Cicero. Capone survived the hit attempt, thanks to a loyal henchman who threw his own body on top of Capone's as the bullets started flying.

Capone began to assume a larger-than-life persona in the eyes of the public, taking his place among other legendary figures of the Roaring Twenties, like baseball

*Bullet-riddled corpses and a pockmarked wall inside Bugs Moran's headquarters, February 14, 1929. Al Capone believed the Saint Valentine's Day Massacre would solve his problems with a rival gang. He hadn't counted on the massive public outrage that ensued from the brutal slayings.*

player Babe Ruth, jazz musician Louis Armstrong, and boxer Jack Dempsey. Capone lived large, throwing around hundred-dollar bills like a farmer scattering seeds. He made the *Guinness Book of World Records* in 1927 for amassing the highest gross income ever by a private citizen in a single year ($105 million). One Christmas he spent more than $100,000 on gifts for friends and family. The fact that he had gotten rich by violent and illegal means was glossed over by a fascinated public. The unpopularity of the federal ban on alcohol fed into a converse appreciation for the men who most fully opposed this law. Capone, who bolstered his public image by spending lavishly and loudly on charity, knew that the foundation of his popularity lay in the general public's disregard for Prohibition laws. "All I ever did was supply a demand that was pretty popular," he said.

With the public behind him and the police force in his back pocket ("Sixty percent of my policemen are in the bootleg business," reported the Chicago chief of police during Capone's reign), there seemed to be little that could stop Capone. But the mob boss's violent tendencies proved to be his undoing. Seeking to deliver a fatal blow to the already seriously weakened O'Bannion gang, which was now headed by Bugs Moran, Capone ordered what became known as the Saint Valentine's Day Massacre. On February 14, 1929, seven men—six members of Moran's inner circle and one hanger-on—were lined up against a wall and shot to death by several of Capone's machine-gun-wielding hoods, who had gained access to Moran's headquarters by posing as police officers.

The gory killings ended the widespread adulation of Capone, as the public awoke to a fact that law enforcement agents and members of the Chicago underworld had known for years. "Only Capone kills like that," uttered gang boss Bugs Moran, the intended target of the Saint Valentine's Day Massacre. Moran had escaped Capone's murderous attack only because he was late for a scheduled meeting.

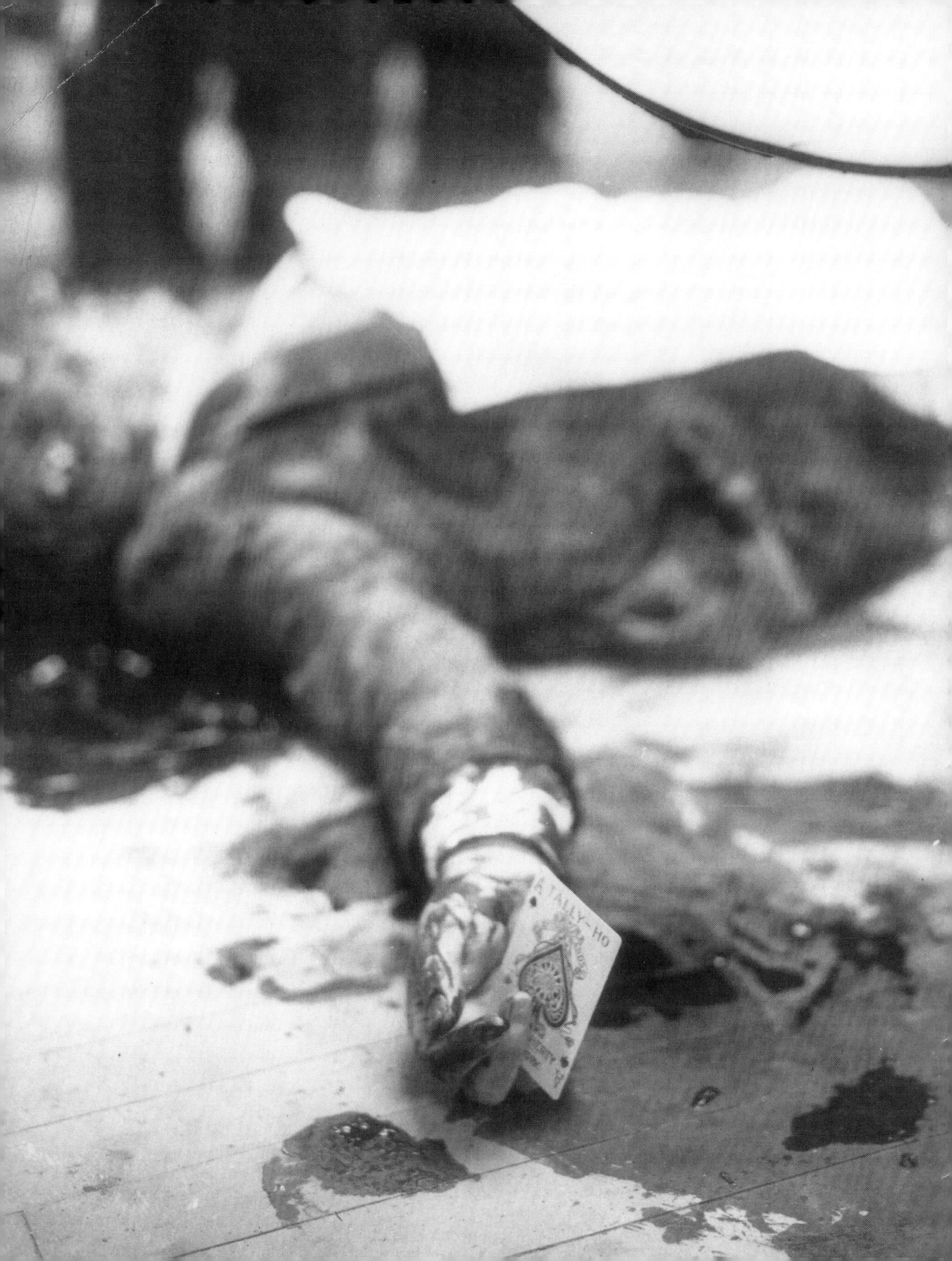
TALLY-HO

# THE MOB RULES

The mob rules: Anyone standing in the way of big profits shall be eliminated; elimination shall be effected through murder. Old World mafioso Joe "the Boss" Masseria was savagely killed at the behest of his lieutenant Lucky Luciano, with whom he had been playing pinochle. Masseria's murder helped pave the way for Luciano's plans for a national criminal syndicate.

The first national meeting between organized crime leaders commenced with Al Capone ripping paintings from the walls of an Atlantic City hotel lobby and throwing them at Atlantic City gang boss Nucky Johnson. Surprisingly, this fracas proved to be the only incident that distinguished the 1929 conference from a normal meeting between powerful industry leaders. Gang bosses forgot old disputes and forged new alliances while brainstorming for ways in which they could work together to achieve higher profits, the goal of all organized crime.

In a striking testament to the atmosphere of cooperation, the conference ended with Capone agreeing to surrender to the authorities. Capone saw, along with everyone else there, that the public outrage caused by the Saint Valentine's Day Massacre could increase the pressure of law enforcement agencies on organized crime in general. President Herbert Hoover himself was said to have been furious at the carnage and to have ordered a crackdown. The gang bosses, Capone included, reasoned that if the most notorious gangster in the country served some time in jail, the widespread public outrage would be quelled.

Capone found, however, that he was still a marked man after serving a 10-month sentence on a minor weapons charge. A group of powerful private businessmen formed with the sole purpose of finding a way to put Capone behind bars for good. The Secret Six, as the group came to be known, funded and oversaw a dogged pursuit and harassment of the Chicago gang boss that was carried out by a special squad of nine law enforcement agents under the command of Eliot Ness. The squad, dubbed "the Untouchables" for their unshakable determination to refuse all bribes, raided Capone's breweries and distilleries and disrupted his liquor-distribution network.

The Secret Six offered a working model of how to battle organized crime effectively. First of all, any fight against organized crime needs to have the kind of money and political clout behind it that the Secret Six enjoyed, because organized crime groups themselves have abundant resources upon which to draw in circumventing the law. Second, law enforcement agents must, like the Untouchables, be above corruption, or organized crime groups will merely bribe their way out of trouble. After his underworld empire had been toppled, Capone himself paid tribute to the dogged determination of his adversaries, saying, "The Secret Six licked the rackets. They licked me. They've made it so there's no money in the game anymore."

In truth, however, the efforts of Internal Revenue Service (IRS) agents had more to do with Capone's downfall than the Secret Six or the Untouchables. The gangster had failed to pay one cent in income taxes on the hundreds of millions of dollars he had raked in over the years, and this oversight caught up with him in 1931, when he was convicted and sentenced to 11 years in prison for income tax evasion.

Capone was not the only flamboyant mobster to go down in the early 1930s. Waxey Gordon was also jailed on tax evasion charges, Legs Diamond was shot to death in his sleep, and Dutch Schultz was murdered in the bathroom of a tavern in Newark, New Jersey. The demise of these high-profile gangsters, coupled with the repeal of Prohibition in 1933, seemed to lend credence to Capone's claim that "there's no money in the game anymore."

In reality, organized crime continued to thrive. The downfall of gangsters like Capone and Gordon, both of whom had been named "Public Enemy Number One" in their respective cities, actually helped organized crime in general by creating an illusion that the illegal industry had been dealt a crippling blow. Decades would pass before this illusion was shattered. In the meantime, organized crime spread its roots deep and wide throughout America.

In the decades after Prohibition, organized crime in America became the domain, primarily, of the American Mafia. The Mafia had originated in Sicily in the 1800s, growing out of the private armies employed by wealthy landowners striving to keep a firm grasp on their property. During the boom in Italian immigration in the late 1800s and early 1900s, the Mafia traveled to the United States. At first, the Mafia in America was no more than a collection of relatively disorganized and unaffiliated gangs, their criminal exploits confined primarily to urban Italian neighborhoods. The true American Mafia was born during Prohibition, when Lucky Luciano, with ample help from Meyer Lansky, orchestrated the murders of the two biggest Old World Mafia bosses in America, Salvatore Maranzano (who had dubbed himself "the Boss of Bosses") and Maranzano's main rival, Joe "the Boss" Masseria.

Maranzano and Masseria were part of the older generation of mobsters referred to disparagingly by Luciano and his brash cohorts as "Mustache Petes" for their outdated style of facial hair. They had been holding on too tightly to Old World dicta that forbade entering into partnerships with gangsters from other ethnic groups (such as Meyer Lansky, a Jew), and they also tended to shy away from doing business beyond the confines of their Italian neighborhoods. Luciano, who had already joined the vast multiethnic criminal network known as the Big Seven Group, generally disregarded any rule, spoken or unspoken, that got in the path of his desire to expand his money-making capabilities.

The elimination of Maranzano and Masseria paved the way for the American Mafia to become fully incorporated into the emerging national crime syndicate. Luciano had envisioned a criminal landscape in which such a syndicate, presided over by a board of directors, would maintain order among the largest organized crime groups, eliminating unnecessary intergang violence and thus maximizing profits. Beginning in the early 1930s, he led a group of organized crime figures in bringing that vision to reality. Criminal territories were established, rules of conduct enunciated, protocol defined. When a member of the syndicate took independent action that threatened the position of other syndicate members, the board—which included such criminal luminaries as Luciano, Frank Costello, Meyer Lansky, and Louis "Lepke" Buchalter—imposed severe punishment, regardless of the offender's position. For example, the board ordered the murder of Dutch Schultz, a founding member of the syndicate, because Schultz would not be dissuaded from his intention to kill Thomas E. Dewey, New York City's district attorney, who had been investigating him. The board members believed, not unreasonably, that the murder of Dewey could only lead to a crackdown on organized crime in general.

Though the syndicate initially comprised criminal organizations from several ethnic groups, the Mafia soon assumed a central position—and dominated organized crime throughout the United States for years after. The powerful Jewish and Irish gangs of the Prohibition era, such as those run by Waxey Gordon and Dion O'Bannion, were unable to survive long after the demise of their leaders. This was not the case with the more streamlined and organized Italian crime groups. When Lucky Luciano was sent to prison in 1936, for example, his longtime associate Frank Costello was there to take over as the head of Luciano's operation.

In hindsight, the American Mafia during the post-Prohibition years has come to be seen as an entity no less organized and hierarchical than a multinational corporation. This view is somewhat inaccurate. In truth the different Mafia "families" across the country pursued their own ends without appealing to a "boss of bosses." But there was extensive cooperation and communication between the different families. Additionally, all the families had access to a certain nationwide service that not only aided the growth of the organized crime industry but also set it apart from other industries. Murder, Incorporated, started in the 1930s by Meyer Lansky and Bugsy Siegel and led during its heyday by Lepke Buchalter and Albert Anastasia, offered killers-for-hire to members of the national crime syndicate and enforced the decisions of the syndicate's board members.

From a business standpoint, this deadly service filled a need, and it did so with great efficiency. Periodically, a mob boss might need someone dead. If his own men did the killing, there was a risk that they might be recognized and lead police back to the mob boss himself, whose motive would usually be apparent to police. Murder, Incorporated killers, on the other hand, came from out of town, murdered their target (whom they didn't know and who didn't know them), and returned to their hometown. They had no overt dealings with the mobster who ordered the killing. Establishing a

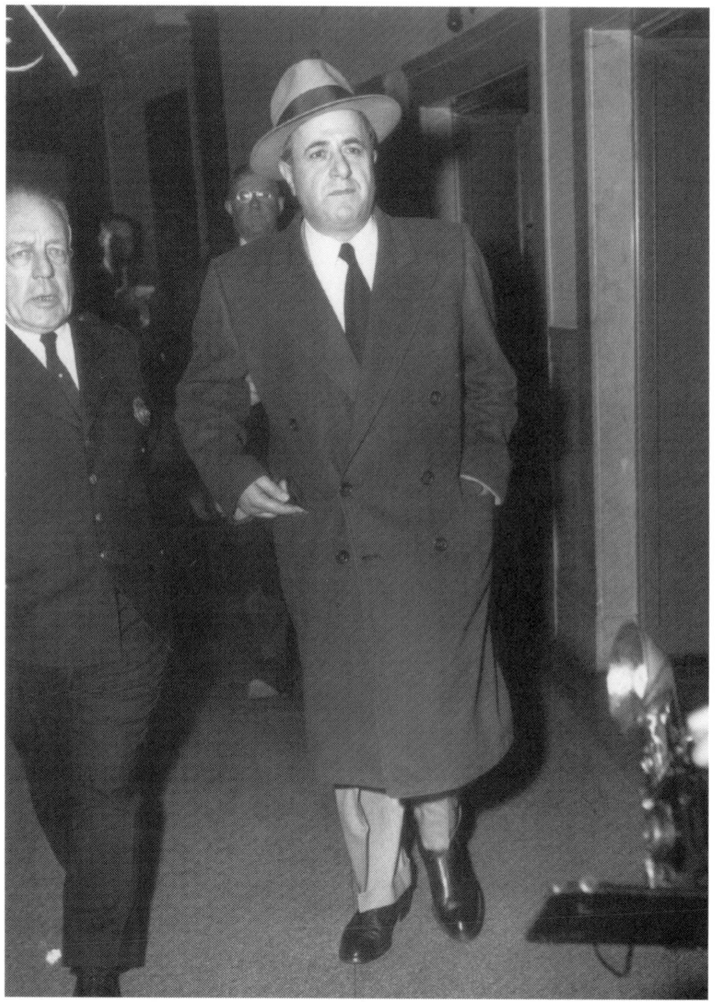

*Murder, Incorporated head Albert Anastasia, believed to have personally murdered at least 50 people, assigned hit men to kill hundreds of others.*

motive and identifying a killer were thus extremely difficult for the police.

An estimated 400 to 500 "contracts"—many ordered by the syndicate's board of directors to enforce discipline—were carried out by the Murder, Incorporated assassins within seven years of its origination. While they waited for an assignment, the hit men drew a regular salary; each successful murder brought a bonus, typically between $1,000 and $5,000. In addition, if one of its killers was arrested, Murder, Incorporated would provide a high-priced lawyer for his defense. The organization even offered a generous benefits package that included life insurance and medical and retirement plans. Syndicate members viewed expenditures on Murder, Incorporated as a cost of doing business in the specialized industry of organized crime.

Despite the existence of shared services such as Murder, Incorporated and general efforts of mob families to cooperate, the American Mafia never achieved the kind of business integration characteristic of multinational corporations, as the public would erroneously come to believe. But the view of the American Mafia as a unified corporation, though flawed, does come far closer to the truth than the publicly stated appraisal of the situation put forth by the federal law enforcement agents of the era. J. Edgar Hoover, head of the Federal Bureau of Investigation (FBI) throughout the American Mafia's strongest years, repeatedly claimed that there was no such thing as organized crime.

One of Hoover's top aides, William C. Sullivan, revealed upon his retirement from the FBI that such a ludicrous claim was made out of fear, saying, "The Mafia is . . . so powerful that entire police forces or even a mayor's office can be under Mafia control. That's why Hoover was afraid to let us tackle it." A recent Hoover biographer, Anthony Summers, claimed that the director's failure to pursue organized crime stemmed from a different kind of fear. In his 1993 book *Official and Confidential,* Summers argued that the Mafia had evidence of Hoover's homosexuality, which the FBI director feared they might release if he vigorously investigated the mob.

Whatever the case, the lack of federal interference eased the rise of the Mafia as it adjusted to the end of Prohibition. The Mafia grabbed a piece of the profits in the newly legal liquor business and more fully diversified its illegal activities, expanding its involvement in loan-sharking operations, prostitution, crooked labor unions, narcotics, and gambling.

In 1950 and 1951, Americans gained an awareness of the doings of organized criminals when Senator Estes Kefauver of Tennessee headed the Senate Special Committee to Investigate Crime in Interstate Commerce. The televised Kefauver Hearings, as they became known, gradually and dramatically put forth a somewhat distorted vision of organized crime in America. In the hearings, organized crime was depicted as the work of dark, sinister invaders from foreign countries. A myth of organized crime was born, which ignored certain important facts. It ignored the fact that crime groups other than those composed of Italians existed. It glossed over the highly important links between crooked politicians, crooked law enforcement agents, and mobsters. It ignored the fact that demand for illegal goods and services is a key part of organized crime's success. It was, in short, a simplified view. With an issue as complex as organized crime, simplification can be dangerous. The myth popularized by the hearings would in certain ways work to help, not hinder, the growth of organized crime. But at least the American public became aware that there was such a thing as organized crime.

The awareness of the magnitude of organized crime in the United States grew in 1957 with the chance discovery, by local police, of a national meeting of mob bosses in Apalachin, New York. With the meeting serving as irrefutable evidence of the existence of a national crime syndicate, the FBI finally had to begin investigating organized crime figures in earnest. At the time of the Apalachin meeting, 400 FBI agents were stationed in New York City for the purpose of rooting out Communist spies, while only four agents were assigned to the investigation of organized crime.

The FBI and other law enforcement agents struggled in their attempts to combat organized crime in the years immediately following the Apalachin meeting. The biggest victory of that era came in 1959, when mob

*Mobster Joe Valachi testifies before the U.S. Senate Permanent Investigations Subcommittee, October 1, 1963. The first major figure to violate the Mafia's code of secrecy, Valachi cast light on the workings of the Cosa Nostra.*

boss Vito Genovese was arrested and sentenced to 15 years in prison for his central role in a multimillion-dollar drug-smuggling operation. But it would later come to light that this seeming triumph for law enforcement had been the product of Mafia infighting: Genovese, after becoming too greedy for power, had been wrapped in a bundle of damning evidence by other mobsters and handed like a gift to federal prosecutors.

The seemingly impenetrable coating of secrecy that surrounded the Mafia finally began to crack in 1963 when a longtime member of the organization, Joe Valachi, stepped forward to speak to the Senate Permanent Investigations Subcommittee. Much of Valachi's testimony was eventually revealed to be the overblown inventions of a low-level mob figure who wasn't privy to the actual facts in such key matters as the formation of the American Mafia near the end of Prohibition. However, Valachi was able to provide useful information on the shadowy culture of the organization he and his fellow mobsters referred to as "La Cosa Nostra" (literally, "our thing"). During his extensive testimony, the gravel-voiced Valachi described an organization that demanded of its members, by penalty of a torturous death, total loyalty and secrecy. It also demanded a very particular occupational skill, one that in many ways defined the Mafia. Valachi referred to this skill when he was asked how he had proved himself worthy of rising in the hierarchy of the organization. "Just kill for them," Valachi replied.

By the end of the 1960s, federal legislators had begun to devise laws to aid in the fight against organized crime. First, in 1968, the Omnibus Crime and Safe Streets Act gave the government the authority, for the first time, to use wiretaps in investigations that were not matters of national security. The law, as critics pointed out, threatened to sacrifice the personal privacy of innocent civilians. But it also began to pay almost immediate dividends as law enforcement agents used wiretaps to learn about the workings of a syndicate that had been closed off to them for decades by *omertà*, the Mafia's virtually unbreakable code of silence.

In 1970, the Racketeer Influenced and Corrupt Organizations Act (RICO), a statute of the Crime Control Act, was passed. RICO made it illegal to own or operate a business that had established a "pattern of racketeering." In other words, any organization proven to be involved in any kind of illegal business on two or more occasions in a span of 10 years was fair game for RICO prosecution. And anyone affiliated with that organization (even its highest-ranking members, who

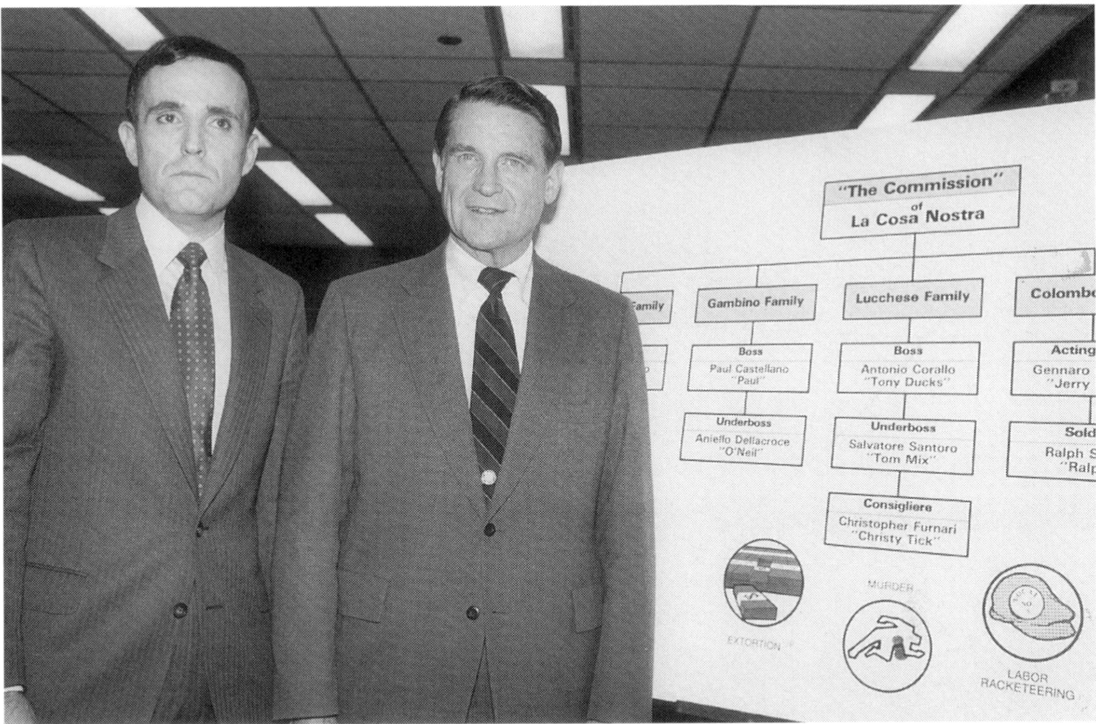


*Prosecutor Rudolph Giuliani (left) and FBI director William Webster pose in front of a Mafia organizational chart. Giuliani's successful prosecution of 16 high-level mobsters led him to speculate about the imminent demise of the Mafia. Such speculation proved premature.*

had in the past often been able to distance themselves from the various crimes they orchestrated) could be snatched up in the RICO prosecution. The new law allowed prosecutors to focus not merely on isolated criminal acts but on entire, wide-ranging criminal enterprises. It was a bold attempt to enable prosecutors to strike at the very roots of organized crime groups.

Years would pass before prosecutors learned how to use RICO effectively, however. In the meantime, the 1970s proved to be an era in which information about the Mafia abounded. Some of the information was legitimate and useful, like that provided by Joe Pistone, a federal agent who posed as a jewel thief named Donnie Brasco and infiltrated the powerful Bonanno crime family for more than five years. Most of the information, however, like that contained in the wildly popular movie *The Godfather*, obscured the actual truths about organized crime with inflated myths. These myths compounded the myths established by the earlier Kefauver Committee to create a widespread belief that organized crime and the Mafia were one and the same. Unfortunately, this public perception seemed to shape law enforcement strategies. Blossoming Asian and Hispanic organized crime groups were widely ignored as politicians and law officers alike bought into the myth that the Mafia was the only organized crime group around.

Focusing on Italian crime groups did, however, pay some dividends in the 1980s, when several effective strategies came together to cripple Mafia activities in New York City. First, the extensive FBI manpower that had been missing in earlier decades was finally deployed, with hundreds of agents investigating members of the various New York City crime families. Second, an investigation into a Mafia drug-smuggling ring became an international one as U.S. agents pooled information with Italian law enforcement. Third, prosecutors finally learned to use RICO to their advantage. The result was the conviction of 16 American and Sicilian mobsters, including a former Sicilian Mafia chief named Gaetano Badalamenti, and the shutting down of a heroin-smuggling pipeline that had brought 1,650 pounds of the drug into the country in the span of five years. Rudy Giuliani, the lead prosecutor in the Pizza Connection case (so called because the mob had used pizzerias as fronts for drug distribution and money laundering), said at the time, "If we continue our efforts, there's not going to be a Mafia in five years."

With the jailing, in 1992, of Gambino family leader John Gotti, generally considered to be the most powerful Mafia boss in the country, Giuliani's claim seemed even more plausible. In truth, the Mafia has not disappeared, though it no longer stands alone atop the American organized crime world. It has been weakened by tenacious federal investigation and prosecution. Also, the Mafia has suffered from having fewer street-tough foot soldiers now that there is no longer a large Italian immigrant population living in poor urban neighborhoods.

But the weakening of the Mafia has not translated into a general weakening of organized crime in this country. As the Mafia's strong central role in the crooked industry gradually declined in the 1970s and 1980s, other crime groups surged. The landscape of American organized crime came to resemble a feeding frenzy in which the lion that killed to start the feast had to make room for a host of equally bloodthirsty jackals, vultures, and hyenas.

CEE-292

# 5.

# "An Empire Based on Murder"

In June of 1985, an FBI wiretap on the phone of Mafia underboss Aniello Dellacroce captured a piece of information that spoke volumes about the changing face of organized crime in America. Previously, when a crime group not affiliated with the Mafia got too big, they paid the Mafia a percentage of their profits or else paid with their lives. This apparently was no longer the case. As FBI agents listened in, Dellacroce told an associate that he needed to pay a 35 percent cut of the profits in his gambling operations to a Cuban gang. The alternative, Dellacroce explained, was a war. The clear implication was that it was a war the Italians could not win.

Historically, organized crime groups in the United States have tended to form around a shared ethnic

*Near Cali, Colombia. The never-ending struggle for a share of the enormously profitable international drug trade has left a trail of murders all over the world.*

identity. The precursors of these groups—street gangs such as the Jewish, Irish, and Italian gangs that sprang up around the country in the 19th century—gave immigrant youths a measure of protection in tough urban neighborhoods and a sense of belonging in a society that marginalized and discriminated against them. It is perhaps not surprising that as the street gangs evolved into purely criminal organizations, they tended to maintain a strong ethnic orientation. Shared backgrounds, customs, and culture promoted trust within the organization.

Ethnically constituted organized crime groups continue to predominate today, although a subtle shift seems to have occurred in the goals of at least some of these groups. Previously, organized crime groups operating in the United States sought an alternative path to the American dream—they wanted to succeed *in* America and *as* Americans. In recent years, organized crime has assumed a more international character. Some of the most powerful groups view the United States as simply the largest market for their illegal goods and services, while they continue to live in—and direct their organizations from—their countries of origin.

By the 1980s, Spanish was spoken in many organized crime circles in the United States. As Aniello Dellacroce's FBI-monitored phone conversation made clear, Latin American organized crime groups had risen to a level of power that in certain locations and criminal pursuits was equal to or greater than that of the Mafia. Ironically, this rise had begun in the 1950s with the ample help of the Mafia. At that time Meyer Lansky, always on the lookout for ways to increase his profits and the profits of his associates, spearheaded the Mafia's expansion into gambling operations in Cuba.

Lansky used Mafia money to forge a tight relationship with Cuban dictator Fulgencio Batista. Batista's willingness to work with Lansky's operation defined an atmosphere of corruption that spread widely throughout the Cuban government and police force as Mafia-run casinos flourished. But Cuba's mobster paradise would prove to be short-lived. Fidel Castro, who led the Communist overthrow of Batista's dictatorship in 1959, actively rid his country of any and all Mafia influences.

The anti-Communist U.S. government was against Castro from the start, which put the government in the unfortunate company of mobsters and corrupt Cuban officials. The Central Intelligence Agency (CIA) used members of Batista's crooked regime in operations designed to overthrow Castro. The operations failed miserably. The failure was compounded when the CIA cut loose all the Cuban nationals it had trained. Now drifting into America were scores of men who had ample ties with the Mafia plus extensive CIA training in the use of automatic weapons and explosives.

One of the first of the CIA-trained Cubans to make a mark in American organized crime was a former vice cop with ties to Meyer Lansky, José Miguel Battle (pronounced BAHT-lay). Battle used the shady alliances he had forged in Cuba to gain a foothold in illegal gambling in both Florida and New York City. Specifically, Battle got involved in the numbers racket, a kind of illegal lottery that thrived in poor urban neighborhoods and that had been a staple industry of organized crime since the late 1800s. By the 1960s, the Mafia had begun a gradual withdrawal from the day-to-day operations of numbers rackets throughout the country. This withdrawal opened up opportunities for newcomers like Battle.

Battle began dispatching CIA-trained enforcers to expand the territory of his numbers operation. These enforcers barged in on independent racketeers running numbers operations out of their storefronts and demanded that they turn over the lion's share of their profits to Battle. Numbers operators who balked at this demand generally paid with their lives. Battle's gang established a reputation for terror by blowing up cars and burning down stores to murder the people who defied them.

Battle's gang, which eventually became known as "the Corporation," used portions of its abundant earnings to bribe politicians in its New York City metropolitan area stronghold of Union City, New Jersey. Union City became a safe haven for the Corporation, allowing Battle to grow ever more ambitious in his criminal pursuits without fear of being brought up on charges. Battle also shielded his illegal operations by setting up a host of legitimate businesses, such as banks, travel agencies, and real estate companies. The profits from his blood-soaked numbers racket could be hidden among the profits of his legal businesses.

The violence of the Corporation grew along with its profits. In the early 1980s, Battle ordered a spree of arson murders in a war with Puerto Rican numbers operators that took the lives of 11 people, including a three-year-old girl and her baby-sitter. A massive public outcry erupted, and Battle, sensing that the police and federal prosecutors would spare no effort to capture the murderers, left the country to further insulate himself from the grisly day-to-day operations of the Corporation. According to law enforcement experts, he continues to run a criminal operation that is the equal of any in America. "I consider Battle the king of illegal gambling in the country," said a Florida organized crime investigator named David Green. "You could take all the mob families in the country and you won't find one as strong as this."

While the Corporation seemed to restrict its illegal dealings to the numbers racket and other forms of illicit gambling, other Cuban gangs grew strong by smuggling and selling illegal narcotics. Cuban drug dealers benefited from the Mafia's partial withdrawal from the drug trade in the 1960s. A series of convictions of powerful Mafia leaders in the late 1950s and early 1960s on

*Gamblers in a Havana casino, 1957. Dictator Fulgencio Batista allowed American mobster Meyer Lansky to establish lucrative gambling rackets for the Mafia in Cuba. Cuban mobsters, in turn, set up shop in the United States following Batista's ouster.*

drug-trafficking charges had the Mafia shying away from the drug trade as never before. This reluctance allowed upstart Cuban gangs to establish a strong foothold in a business that would prove to be the most explosively profitable organized crime racket since the Prohibition-era liquor trade.

Prohibition, which had been marked by massive violence and by the widespread transformation of penniless hoodlums into millionaires, found a mirror image in the burgeoning drug trade of the 1960s. Cuban gangsters got rich as they seized control of the flow of cocaine and marijuana from Latin American countries. A more frightening echo of Prohibition occurred in the 1970s, when an immensely powerful organized crime group from Colombia, the Medellín cocaine cartel, muscled in on the Cuban drug racket in Florida. In comparison with the Medellín cartel, America's Prohibition-era gangsters might seem like wayward boys; the Colombian cocaine barons displayed a seemingly limitless capacity for murderous violence. The profits available in Prohibition had fostered the growth of American organized crime into a powerful nationwide industry. The size and scope of the Medellín cartel suggested that the profits available in the drug trade had greatly helped organized crime expand into a thoroughly *international* industry.

The Medellín cartel was surpassed in the early 1980s by the even more powerful Colombian criminal organization known as the Cali cartel. The Cali cartel, which was run with the same efficiency and strict focus on bottom-line economics as a major multinational corporation, saw that it was ultimately bad for business to engage in the kind of street-level gang-war violence that the Medellín cartel had become famous for. They separated themselves from the street-level "dirty work" by pulling out of the business of drug distribution in the United States. They continued to supply drugs (mainly cocaine) to other Latin American organized crime groups, in effect letting these groups do the dirty work while they continued to pull in massive profits.

The Cali cartel did business with Cuban gangs and, on the West Coast particularly, with Mexican gangs. But by the 1980s, the primary players in street-level distribution of cocaine in the United States were gangsters from the Dominican Republic. The extent of involvement of Dominican gangsters in the drug trade could be seen most clearly by the amount of drugs passing through their hands—in one drug bust authorities found 5.5 *tons* of cocaine at a warehouse owned by a Dominican drug lord named Ramón Velásquez.

In New York City, Dominican gangs battled ferociously among themselves and with other ethnic gangs for a share of the skyrocketing profits, transforming the Dominican neighborhood of Washington Heights into a war zone. In 1992 alone, 122 murders were committed there, making it the most dangerous neighborhood in the city. Gangs came and went quickly, their leaders either thrown in jail or murdered by other gangs. But the drug trade itself always continued on, unaffected. Frustrated law enforcement officials blame this seeming invincibility on the sheer numbers of young hoodlums attracted to the promise of big money in the cocaine racket.

"They're coming in here in droves," said a Hartford, Connecticut, police officer named Norberto Huertas. "We make arrests at a location, and they have replacements there in an hour."

An even bigger factor in the continued strength of the cocaine business is that the flow of the drug into the United States never slows. When police officers like Norberto Huertas arrest a street-level drug dealer in Hartford, Connecticut, it affects the nationwide drug trade about as much as the plucking of a single blade of grass would affect the overall health of a vast field.

*Pablo Escobar Gaviria, one of the leaders of Colombia's ultraviolent Medellín cocaine cartel. Tired of being pursued, however half-heartedly, by Colombian law enforcement, Escobar negotiated his surrender and "punishment." He constructed a comfortably appointed prison to house himself and other Medellín associates for brief jail terms. When "prison" life began to lose its appeal, Escobar simply walked out.*

The individual blades of grass—the foot soldiers of street gangs—form the final link in the distribution chain of an industry that generates incredible profits: they sell the illegal drugs to consumers on the street. But although they run a high risk of being arrested or targeted for violence, their monetary compensation is typically quite low. A 1998 study by University of Chicago economist Steven Levitt and Harvard University sociologist Sudhir Venkatesh found that a drug gang's street-level pushers can expect to make slightly over three dollars per hour. That reality seems to have been largely lost on aspiring gang members and the news media, who continue to view street-level drug pushing as a lucrative enterprise.

Not surprisingly, the financial rewards of organized crime have always accrued disproportionately to those at the top of the hierarchy. Nonetheless, there has never been a dearth of street-gang members willing to perform the many dangerous tasks without which organized crime groups could not function: distributing illegal products to consumers, intimidating the targets of extortion and protection rackets, fighting the "soldiers" of rival groups, murder.

The powerful Colombian cocaine cartels—the ultimate beneficiaries of much street-level gang activity in the United States—made sure to remain beyond the reach of U.S. law enforcement when they terrorized Colombian legislators into rewriting their nation's constitution in 1991. In the five years before the revision of Colombia's fundamental government document, the cartels seized their country by the throat, assassinating more than 1,000 police officers and public officials. The result of this reign of terror was a new constitution that made it impossible to extradite criminals from Colombia. In other words, Colombian drug traffickers could not be forced to stand trial in the United States, no matter how big a part they played in the criminal racket that has left a trail of murders across America.

The ability of the drug cartel leaders to have their country's constitution rewritten was merely the most galling of the many testaments to their vast power in Colombia. The cartels are able to influence most matters of state that affect them by using their ample connections in the government. By bribing phone company officials, the cartels set up a system in which they could listen in on any phone conversation in the country, thus making it even more difficult for honest Colombian law enforcement agents to move against them. On the rare occasion that a cartel leader is convicted of a crime, his imprisonment more closely resembles a vacation than any kind of significant punishment. A former cartel member, in testimony to a

U.S. Senate subcommittee on international crime, summed up the state of affairs in Colombia, saying, "We have the illusion of democracy, but the [Cali] supercartel controls it."

As democracy in Colombia decreases, the Colombian drug-trafficking industry grows stronger. Business is booming, to say the least. In one instance, police discovered $150 million that the Cali cartel had buried in the ground. Usually, the cartel puts its swelling profits to better use, funneling them back into the business like any other multinational corporation would. The cartel employs an estimated 24,000 people full time, from growers, smugglers, and distributors of narcotics to high-priced accountants, lawyers, chemists, and, of course, assassins.

The Colombian cartels do business all over the world, and nowhere so much as in the United States, where they control an estimated 80 percent of the thriving cocaine market. They have become such complex and powerful organizations that they resemble a common street gang about as closely as the Coca-Cola corporation resembles a five-year-old kid's lemonade stand. This level of complexity protects the top cartel members from being touched by the violence and despair that the illegal narcotics industry feeds on. In reality, the hands of the cartel leaders are bloodier than those of the most violent street-gang leader. As Senator John Kerry pointed out in his book *The New War*, "The Cali cartel . . . is an empire based on murder and the cocaine-induced destruction of the human spirit."

ART
NOVELTIES
JEWELRY
PELL ST
ONE - WAY
18 ORANGEADE & ICE CREAM SODA 18
HOY KEE
-18-
BILLIARDS
波樓
海記

# 6.

# A "Super Mafia" Grows in Chinatown

Police outside a pool hall in Chinatown where a tong war shoot-out had wounded seven, 1930. Tong wars, which had erupted periodically throughout the first three decades of the 20th century, subsided in the 1930s, only to rage anew beginning in the 1960s.

In 1986, a Chinese woman was stopped at Kennedy Airport in New York City as she tried to carry into the United States picture frames with heroin hidden inside them. The following year, customs officials discovered 165 pounds of heroin and a million dollars in cash at Kennedy. Heroin was found inside hollowed-out rubber tires, in shipments of umbrellas, and in smaller quantities being carried through personally by Chinese men and women. In Boston in 1988, authorities seized a cargo of 183 pounds of heroin that had been secreted inside a machine used to wash bean sprouts. It would later be revealed that the shipment was part of a heroin pipeline that had dumped more than 1,700 pounds of the drug into the United States in a span of five years.

In the late 1980s, the ample evidence of a connection between the Chinese underworld and the obviously booming heroin trade led politicians and investigators to begin seriously considering the problem of Asian organized crime. On top of their extensive involvement in heroin smuggling, the Asian organized crime groups were involved in illegal gambling rackets, widespread extortion, prostitution, loan-sharking, home invasion robberies, and the smuggling into the United States of illegal aliens. Senator Joseph Biden, speaking before the Senate Judiciary Committee in 1990, referred to Asian organized crime groups as a potential "super Mafia . . . [that poses] a vast and frightening threat to our cities and communities." Biden predicted that Asian organized crime would be "the dominant organized crime force in this country by the middle of the next decade."

Biden's words of warning may have come too late. By 1990, the power and influence of Asian organized crime groups, particularly Chinese organized crime groups, had been growing exponentially in the United States for over two decades. As often seems to happen in the fight against organized crime, politicians and law enforcement got involved well after the criminals had sunk the roots of their violent operations deep into American soil.

The history of Chinese organized crime dates back to the middle of the 17th century, when resistance groups that came to be known as triads formed in China to combat the Mongol invaders who had taken over the country. The triads were concerned at first with acting as a kind of local government to protect their communities from abusive imperial rulers. Initially, the triads engaged in criminal activities to fund their more benevolent pursuits, but over time these benevolent pursuits were largely forgotten and criminal activities became an end in themselves.

Some triad members were scattered in among the throng of hard-working peasants that made up the first surge of Chinese immigration to America in the gold rush era of the mid-19th century. These seasoned felons lent a criminal undertone to the organizations known as

*A turn-of-the-century Chinese grocery store in San Francisco. Tongs arose to protect Chinese immigrants in a frequently hostile U.S. society. But they also ran virtually all the criminal activities in Chinese neighborhoods.*

tongs, which arose primarily as a reaction to the racism that the Chinese immigrants met with in America. The tongs, acting as a kind of unofficial neighborhood police force, offered some measure of protection and stability for immigrants finding themselves in a menacing new world. But they also controlled virtually every illegal enterprise in the immigrant community, running gambling halls, opium dens, and prostitution rings. Also, conflicts between rival tongs frequently turned the Chinese neighborhoods into war zones. Between 1905 and 1906, for example, 50 people died as a result of a battle between the On Leong tong and the Hip Sing tong in New York City.

The tong wars flared up routinely until the early 1930s, when the U.S. Attorney in Manhattan made a concerted effort to put a stop to them. By that time the thriving criminal economy had began to slow down anyway. The population of Chinese immigrant communities tapered off throughout the middle decades of the 20th century as a result of the racist quota laws passed in 1924 to keep Chinese immigration to a bare minimum.

These laws were overridden by the Immigration and Naturalization Act of 1965, which abolished all national quota systems. The ensuing boom in Chinese immigration breathed new life into cities across the country, enriching and enlivening American culture and commerce. It also, however, catalyzed a rebirth of Chinese organized crime. The reasons for this rebirth were relatively simple. "More people meant more gamblers," observed Gwen Kinkead in her 1992 book *Chinatown: Portrait of a Closed Society,* "and the tongs needed muscle to watch the pots."

The tongs hired members of the street gangs that had begun to spring up in Chinatowns all over the country. The gangs had begun in much the same way as Irish, Italian, and Jewish street gangs had in the middle to late 19th century, with adolescents in a strange and often hostile new environment coming together for the purpose of self-protection. These street gangs grew stronger with the backing of the tongs, which used them not only to guard the money generated by their gambling operations, but also to intimidate members of the Chinese business community who were reluctant to fall in line with the tongs' wishes. In return for helping the tongs, the street gangs received steady money (which in turn helped increase their ranks), plus high-priced lawyers when they got into trouble with the law. The support of the tongs encouraged street gangs to branch off into their own criminal endeavors, and soon they were on the brink of becoming powerful organized crime groups in their own right.

*The Mekong River, Laos, 1967. In an effort to raise money to combat Communist insurgencies in Southeast Asia during the 1960s, CIA agents transformed the area known as the Golden Triangle into a major producer of heroin.*

In the early 1970s, the street gangs and the tongs rose to a new level of involvement in organized crime, aided by their ability to take advantage of a situation as ripe with criminal possibilities as Prohibition had been. At that time, the U.S. government was expending a tremendous amount of money and manpower to shut down what was then the key heroin-smuggling route into America, known as the French Connection. But stopping the French Connection did not stop heroin from entering the United States. In fact, it prompted the opening of several new pipelines, which in turn increased the quantity and the level of purity of the heroin coming into the country.

One of the primary heroin-smuggling connections started in an area in Southeast Asia known as the Golden Triangle. All heroin that came out of the Golden Triangle was the property of powerful Chinese triads based in Hong Kong, who were in turn connected with tongs and gangs in the United States. The heroin-smuggling operation that began in the 1970s not only generated massive amounts of money for Chinese crime groups in America, but also helped build these groups into powerful syndicates with strong and far-ranging international connections.

The efforts to curtail Chinese organized crime in America lagged behind the feverish expansion of the various tongs and gangs. In New York City (which is, along with San Francisco, one of the two U.S. centers of Chinese organized crime), some members of the city police department sensed in the 1970s that they had more than they could handle alone in Chinatown. But, as had happened years earlier with the Mafia, the FBI turned a blind eye on the problem. "We tried like hell to get the Feds interested, but they ignored us," said former police detective Neil Mauriello. "They didn't want to be bothered by gangs."

More disturbing than the negligence of the FBI was the fact that the Golden Triangle—the source of heroin that played such a major part in the strengthening of Chinese organized crime groups—had been built into a heroin-producing juggernaut with ample help from the CIA. In the early 1960s, CIA operatives in Southeast Asia raised money for their fight against Communist insurrection by participating fully in the transport of drugs out of the Golden Triangle. As Dennis J. Kenney and James O. Finckenauer wrote in their 1995 book *Organized Crime in America*, "By the mid-1960s, with CIA complicity, the Laotian drug trade had grown from a small one, meeting the demands in its own cities, to a self-contained industry—feeding chemists in Hong Kong for export throughout the world."

The high profits available in the drug-smuggling trade soon led to violent battles in the Chinese underworld, as street gangs and tongs alike grasped for a bigger share of the business. The similarity of the increasingly bloody Chinatown gunplay to gangland violence during the Prohibition era was never clearer than in the aftermath of the shoot-out at the Golden Dragon restaurant in San Francisco on September 4, 1977, in which 5 people were killed and 11 others injured. The carnage reminded some observers of Al Capone's Saint Valentine's Day Massacre, but in one galling respect the Golden Dragon killings were even worse: though the shoot-out stemmed from a conflict between two rival gangs, none of the 16 people shot were gang members. Everyone in the line of fire was an innocent bystander.

The Golden Dragon massacre triggered the formation of a San Francisco Police Department task force designed to address the problem of Chinese organized crime. The biggest obstacle investigators and prosecutors faced in San Francisco and elsewhere in their attempts to put members of Chinese organized crime groups behind bars was coming up with witnesses. Chinatown residents, aware of the way tongs and gangs exacted revenge on anyone who crossed them, almost without exception chose to see no evil, hear no evil, and, most of all, speak no evil. "It's a very complicated problem—the Chinese are deeply frightened," said Nancy Ryan, the chief of the Trial Division in the Manhattan District Attorney's office. "They know there are armed thugs on the street and they can't have twenty-four hour police protection."

The problem is compounded by the fact that many Chinese immigrants have been taught from a young age to distrust public officials. As a result, Chinese neighborhoods remain cut off from the outside world, seeming like insular kingdoms ruled forcefully by tong leaders and street thugs. In many cases, Chinatown denizens look with the utmost regard upon the powerful men in their neighborhood. "They're not looked down on: they're always against the government, which

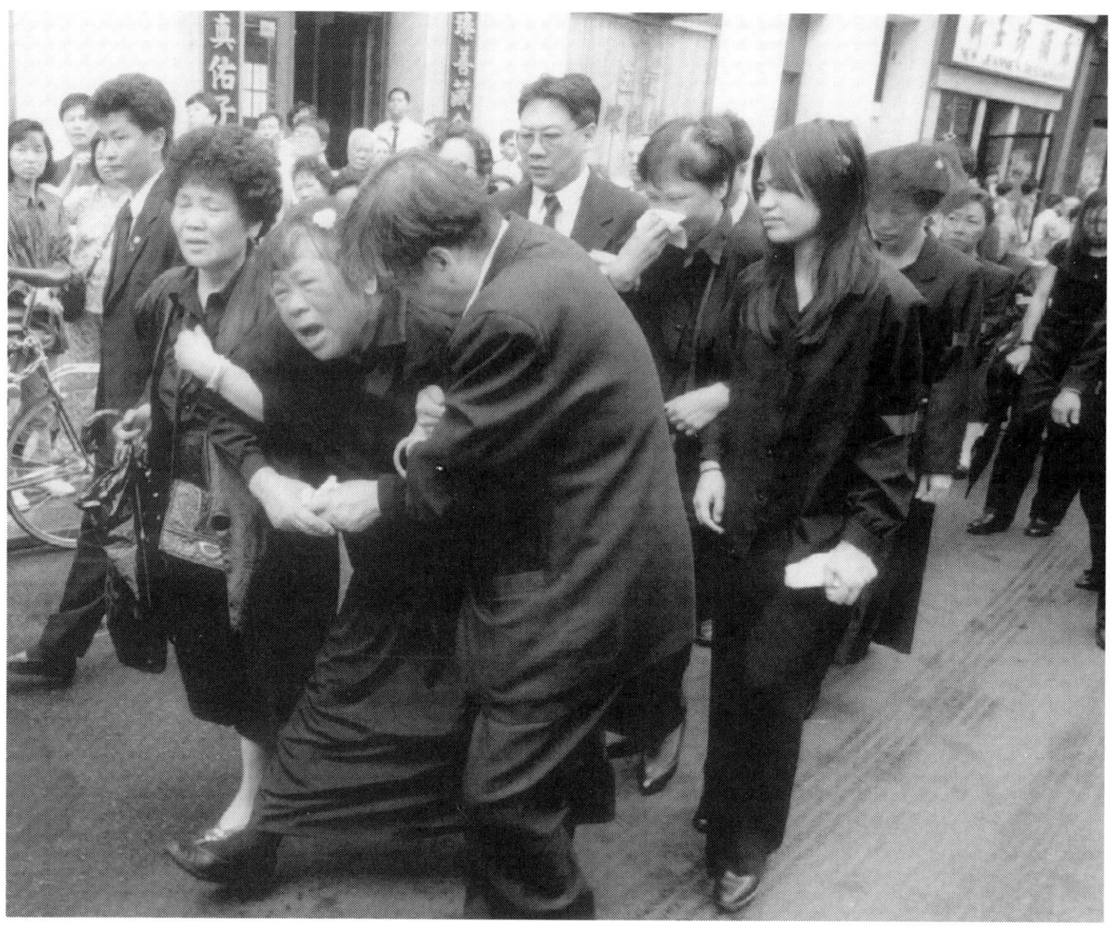

*Benny Ong's funeral procession through New York's Chinatown. The huge outpouring of respect for Ong came despite his well-known status as the leader of Chinese organized crime in New York.*

in Chinese history is always corrupt," points out Taiwanese journalist Quo Chen.

This was never more clear than during the funeral procession of the longtime leader of the Hip Sing tong in 1994. Before rising to the top of organized crime in New York City's Chinatown, Benny Ong had spent 17 years in prison for second-degree murder, and, after becoming the so-called godfather of Chinatown, he had skimmed off the top of every illegal extortion ring, gambling racket, and loan-sharking operation in the neighborhood. Still, as his coffin was carried through Chinatown, thousands of residents crowded the streets to pay their respects to Ong. Ong had known something about how respect works in Chinatown. In 1982, after an associate had tried to double-cross him and take away some of his power in the neighborhood, Ong approved a retaliatory strike on the associate that left three men dead while injuring eight others. "Sixty year I build up respect," Ong said, "and he think he knock me down in one day?"

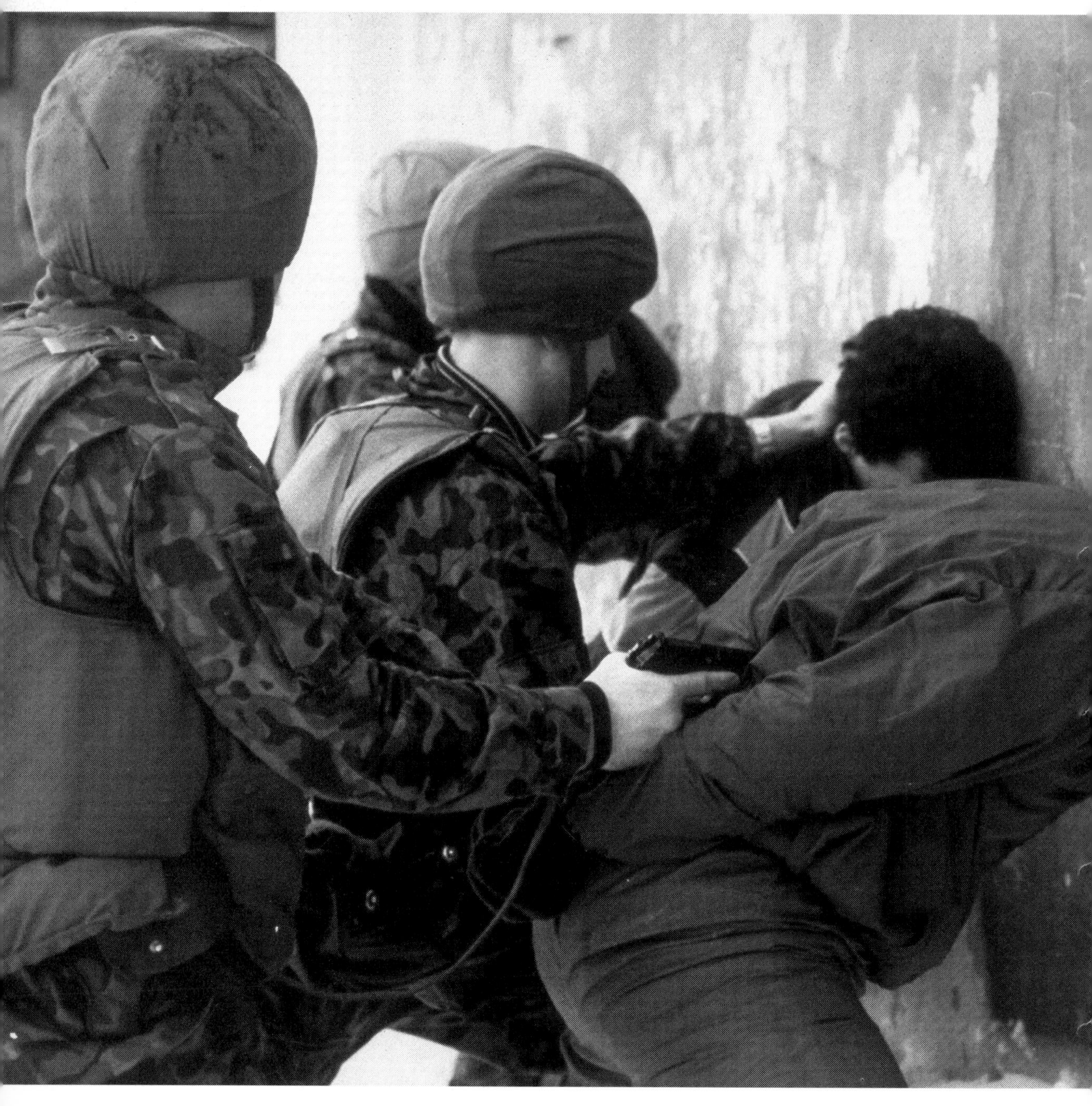

# "They'll Steal Everything"

By the time he had become the boss of the powerful Gambino crime family, few things excited John Gotti more than learning about a new way to make money. In 1986, when Gotti learned of a lucrative fuel-tax scam run by Russian mobsters, he reacted as though he had just been told that someone had discovered how to grow thousand-dollar bills on a tree. "I gotta do it right now!" he exclaimed. "Right now I gotta do it!"

The subsequent involvement of Gotti's organization with the scam led federal investigators to seriously consider, for the first time, the full-scale emergence of a new organized crime power in the United States. A captain in Gotti's outfit, Anthony Morelli, was busted

*Specially trained Russian police arrest organized crime suspects in Moscow. Years of surviving brutal Soviet treatment molded Russian criminal groups into some of the toughest in the world. The demise of the U.S.S.R. set those groups loose on the world.*

in 1993 for his central role in a fuel-tax scam that had siphoned over $100 million from the federal government. Also arrested in the FBI sting operation were six Russians. This was only the tip of the iceberg as far as Russian involvement in fuel-tax scams was concerned. When tax laws were changed in 1994 to make the fuel-tax scam impossible, federal officials, judging that the money that had previously been falling into the hands of Russian gangsters would now be going where it was supposed to, estimated that the government's yearly revenue would increase by $1.3 billion.

The billion-dollar fuel-tax scams were merely a part of the various operations masterminded by Russian criminal groups as they rose to a prominent position in the American criminal underworld in the 1980s. Other rackets included credit card scams, extortion, counterfeiting, prostitution, loan-sharking, and the smuggling and sale of illegal narcotics. The mixture of violence, innovation, and sophistication exhibited by these relative newcomers prompted FBI director Louis Freeh to declare in 1992 that Russian crime groups constituted "the fastest growing criminal organization in the United States."

In 1994, Freeh set up an FBI "legal attaché," or liaison, office in Russia, showing that he understood the unique nature of Russian organized crime in America. Unlike Chinese and Italian organized crime in the United States, which had their primary roots in the street gangs that formed in poor immigrant neighborhoods, Russian organized crime came to American shores fully formed. The roots are in Russian soil. Freeh realized that to act effectively against the Russian mobsters in the United States, he had to work with Russian law enforcement and to understand both the history and the present state of organized crime in Russia.

From 1917 until 1991, organized criminal activity existed at a relatively low yet steady level in Russia. This period, during which Russia was bound together

*Shoppers in Brighton Beach, the Brooklyn neighborhood that is home to a quarter of America's 200,000 recent Russian immigrants. It's also a center of the Russian mob.*

with smaller surrounding countries into the Union of Soviet Socialist Republics (U.S.S.R.), was marked by an extremely repressive and powerful central government that suppressed the personal freedom of most Soviet citizens. At the same time, the repressive Soviet state was able to keep organized crime in check with severe restrictions on transportation, communication, and the ownership of weapons. Criminals couldn't talk on the phone without the government listening in; they could seldom move from place to place without the government knowing about it; and they couldn't get their hands on the kind of weaponry that would have allowed them to forcibly expand their illegal operations.

*FBI director Louis Freeh. Freeh established an FBI liaison office in Moscow to combat the global threat of Russian organized crime.*

Organized crime activity was restricted to the selling of hard-to-find consumer goods on the black market. The men who ran the black market in the U.S.S.R. eventually formed into a tightly knit criminal organization known as *vorovskoi mir*, or "thieves' world." The harsh difficulties of doing illegal business in the U.S.S.R. shaped the group of leaders of the thieves' world (known as "thieves-in-law") the way fire helps shape a sword: they emerged sharp and deadly.

One difficulty for the criminals derived from the ubiquitous official checkpoints that restricted any unauthorized movement from place to place. To move about freely, the thieves-in-law had to become experts at forging official documents. Official documents were also needed to work, to buy consumer goods, and to get medical care, among many other things. The thieves-in-law learned how to fake their way through every level of the vast government-run system. Their skills at forgery, counterfeiting, and dealing with a vast bureaucracy intent on stopping them would serve them well in the legion of complex scams they embarked upon once they reached the United States.

The know-how of the thieves-in-law was augmented by the toughness they developed under the merciless Soviet regime. A New York City police detective, investigating Russian criminal activity in the 1980s, was among the first Americans to learn about this toughness and the benefits it would give the Russian mobsters in their adopted country. The detective recalled a fruitless questioning session with one of the thieves-in-law, saying, "[His] leg looked like a pretzel. It was broken in a dozen places in a Soviet prison. He showed it off and said, 'You're going to do worse to me?' "

Russian mobsters began filtering into the United States amid a boom in Russian immigration that began in the mid-1970s. At first, Russian criminal activity in America was restricted to a series of low-level swindles, but soon enough the characteristic toughness and brutality of the thieves-in-law began to emerge. In Brighton Beach, a New York City neighborhood that is home to a quarter of the 200,000 recent Russian immigrants living in the United States, a powerful Russian mob leader named Evsei Agron seized control of the criminal rackets with the kind of blunt violence that made Al Capone rich. Agron routinely used a sharply pointed cattle prod to extract money from local businessmen, and on one occasion he extorted $15,000 from a fellow émigré by threatening to kill his daughter on her wedding day.

As more of the highly skilled thieves-in-law made their way to the West, Russian organized crime in the United States evolved to include more complex and lucrative enterprises. Evsei Agron's right-hand man, Marat Balagula, a former U.S.S.R. black market specialist with advanced degrees in business and economics, was at the forefront of these changes, pioneering the fuel-tax scam that so fully caught the attention of John Gotti. When Agron was murdered in 1985, Balagula seamlessly took over the reins of his former boss's operations. Balagula's takeover, reminiscent of Johnny Torrio's blood-soaked ascension to power in Chicago at the beginning of Prohibition, signaled that Russian organized crime had fully arrived in the United States. If one boss goes down, another is there to take his place. "Balagula moved into Agron's shoes in all respects," observed IRS investigator Joel Campanella. "This is the classic type of thing you see when a traditional organized crime boss dies."

In the mid-1980s, Russian organized crime got an unexpected boost when Soviet leader Mikhail Gorbachev loosened the government's strict control over the economy. Gorbachev wanted the ailing Russian economy to become more like the healthier economies of Western countries, where private citizens could own businesses. Unfortunately, the thieves-in-law had both the money and the muscle to hijack Gorbachev's admirable plan. They grabbed a huge portion of the blossoming private economy, using their black market funds to get started while simultaneously employing violence and the threat of violence to either scare other investors and entrepreneurs away or force them into partnerships with the criminals. It was the beginning of a widespread infiltration of a criminal element into the economy. At present, an estimated 70 to 80 percent of Russia's private economy is tied to criminal operations.

The increasingly powerful Russian mobsters were again in a good position to profit from political changes in the late 1980s, when the once-powerful Soviet government began to crumble. In 1991, when the U.S.S.R. was dissolved, it marked the end of decades of repressive, authoritarian rule. But it also marked the end of any significant checks on the growth of organized crime in Russia. From 1990 to 1994, the number of organized crime groups identified by the Russian government rose from 785 to 5,691. By 1996, the number had risen to over 8,000.

As the Soviet system collapsed, Russian mobsters advanced from the fringes of their society to a place very near the center. In the chaotic aftermath of the breakup of the U.S.S.R., Russian society in general began to think in a way that a gangster like John Gotti would find familiar. "Now, we have wild democracy," said Aslambek Aslakanov, the head of Russia's Parliamentary Committee on Law and Order, "an epidemic of seizing everything in sight, of getting rich at any cost."

The "thieves' world" soon swelled to include a frightening array of newcomers, from street kids eager to make quick money to suddenly unemployed government scientists willing to help upgrade the Russian mob's technological capabilities. Many soldiers walked away from the crumbling Russian Army to better-paying jobs with Russian gangs. Some higher-ranking officers joined the payrolls of Russian mobsters while remaining in the Russian Army in order to direct gas, weapons, and vehicles into the hands of their new criminal employers. The thieves' world gained scores of frightening allies when the government cut back severely on the ranks of the notoriously vicious Soviet secret police force, the KGB. Many of the 100,000 agents who were turned loose offered their intelligence, international contacts, and penchant for brutality to the Russian gangs. In doing so they extended both the effectiveness and the reach of Russian criminal operations.

Almost instantaneously, Russian organized crime exploded into a worldwide phenomenon. In 1994, FBI chief Louis Freeh reported before a congressional committee that Russian gangs had established operations in 29 countries throughout the world. Two years later, Freeh reported that the number had been upped to 50 countries. What was primarily Russia's problem has become a problem large enough to concern everyone in the world. "Now we've opened the gates, and this is very dangerous for the world," said Boris Uvarov, a Russian crime investigator, referring to the loosening of border controls that occurred after the demise of the U.S.S.R. "America is getting Russian criminals; Europe is getting Russian criminals. They'll steal everything. You people in the West don't know our Mafia yet; you will, you will."

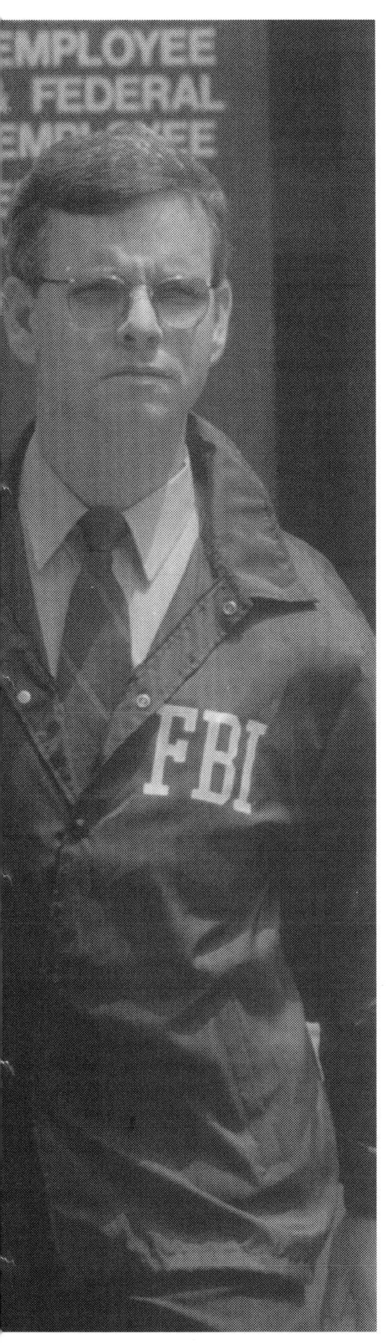


8.

# Who Is Minding the Store?

In 1991, a Russian mobster named Vyacheslav Ivankov bribed his way out of a prison in Siberia. Two years later, fleeing Russian authorities, Ivankov left his home country for a nation that beckoned more and more to gangsters all over the world as a land of seemingly boundless opportunity. These international criminals, according to Philadelphia police investigator John Gallo, are increasingly of the opinion that "the U.S. is like a big candy store with no one minding the store." Ivankov came to the United States to grab some of that candy, unaware that this time someone happened to be watching.

The FBI had learned of Ivankov's migration to the United States through a blossoming dialogue with Russian law enforcement. The FBI could have had

*FBI agents arrest Vyacheslav Ivankov, who some law enforcement officials believe had been sent to the United States "to take control of North America for a Russian crime group."*

Ivankov deported immediately for visa application violations but decided not to, hoping that by observing his movements agents could learn more about the nature of Russian organized crime in the United States. While watching the newcomer build up a fearsome gang in Brighton Beach and forge alliances with Russian organized crime groups all over the United States and Canada, law enforcement agents came to believe, according to one high-ranking official, "that he has been sent here to take control of North America for a Russian crime group."

The authorities foiled Ivankov's plans in 1995 by charging and convicting him in a $3.5 million extortion scheme. The successful way in which the FBI dealt with the would-be king of the Russian-American mob served as a model for combating the increasingly international operations of organized crime groups. First of all, as in a growing number of successful organized crime prosecutions, federal wiretaps provided the evidence needed to put Ivankov in jail.

More important, Ivankov's demise stemmed from the collaboration of American law enforcement agents with their counterparts in a foreign country. This kind of international cooperation, slower to evolve than the international cooperation of organized crime groups, is necessary if the expanding worldwide crime industry is to be kept in check. The events of the latter stages of Prohibition, in which gangs all over the United States began to ally themselves, appear to be repeating themselves on a much larger scale. One organized crime operation discovered in the early 1990s revealed partnerships between gangsters in Pakistan, Africa, Israel, eastern Europe, and Latin America. Other investigations have suggested ties between Colombian drug cartels and organized crime groups in both Italy and Russia, as well as links between the Nigerian drug traffickers, Chinese triads, and the powerful Japanese criminal organizations known as *yakuza*.

Differences between various national governments have hindered the development of worldwide cooperation among law enforcement agencies. The depth of this problem can be seen even within the United States, where separate branches of law enforcement, such as the FBI and the Drug Enforcement Agency (DEA), have repeatedly proven unwilling to share information and work together in criminal investigations. While philosophical differences, jealousy, and outright animosity between law enforcement agencies both in the United States and around the world get in the way of effective investigations, criminal organizations continue to cluster together around the common goal of increased profits.

Organized crime groups are awash in money, which greatly complicates law enforcement's efforts to put them out of business. Huge profits mean crime groups can acquire advanced technology to protect themselves and further their illegal enterprises. The Colombian drug cartels, for example, developed sophisticated computer programs to track the movements of U.S. customs agents; their communications networks use state-of-the-art encryption technology and their own satellite links to prevent messages from being intercepted; they even have a small fleet of remote-controlled submarines, each of which can carry several tons of cocaine more than 1,000 miles. Huge profits also allow organized crime groups to hire top-flight professionals to help keep their organizations intact and in the black: retired officers from the world's best intelligence services to consult on matters of security and counterintelligence, bankers to launder illegally obtained money, accountants to manage the complex flow of expenditures and profits, economists to expand market share. Indeed, some experts believe that marketing specialists employed by the Colombian drug cartels were responsible for the development of crack cocaine. That pernicious product, the experts feel, was designed expressly by the

*Above: When the freighter* Golden Venture *ran aground off Long Island, New York, authorities discovered the existence of a booming business: the smuggling of Fujianese illegal immigrants. Opposite page: A labor investigator questions a young Fujianese garment worker. Fujianese smugglers forced illegal immigrants who could not pay for their passage to assemble clothing under slave-labor conditions.*

Colombians as a cheap (but exceedingly addictive) high for America's urban poor, who could not afford the more expensive powder cocaine.

The ongoing quest for ever-larger illicit profits causes further problems for law enforcement by creating a seemingly endless variety of criminal rackets. Just when investigators learn the workings of one criminal operation, another new way to make dirty money evolves. For example, in the early 1990s, just as investigators and prosecutors were gaining some measure of control over the world of organized crime in New York City's Chinatown, a fearsome new power arose in the form of gangs from the Chinese province of Fujian. These Fujianese gangsters built their empire by turning the smuggling of illegal aliens into the United States into a ruthless, high-profit business.

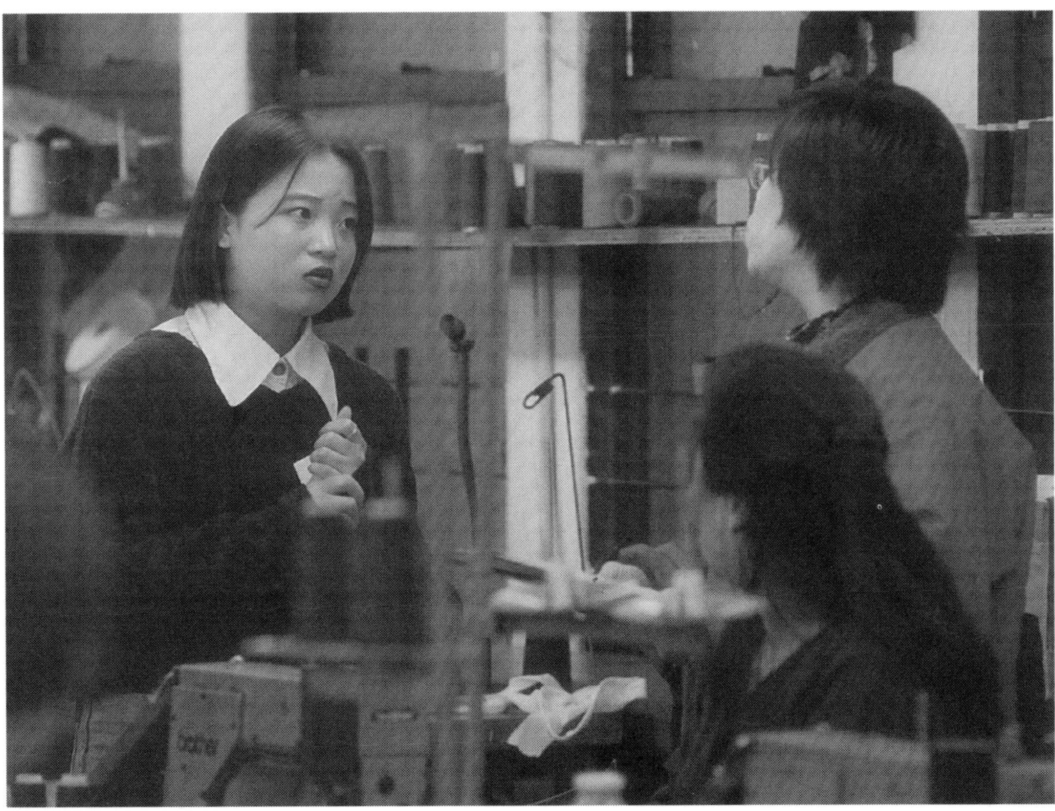

The gangsters packed people by the hundreds into the holds of freight ships headed for the United States. The operation continued undetected until 1993, when a ship called the *Golden Venture*, carrying 300 illegal aliens, ran aground off the coast of Long Island in New York. Investigations prompted by the obvious suffering endured by the passengers on the *Golden Venture* revealed chilling facts about the operation. For one thing, immigrants unable to pay the exorbitant fees demanded by the Fujianese gangsters were held upon arrival in America in crowded, prisonlike cells and forced to perform slave labor.

The fact that organized crime groups will stop short of nothing in their never-ending quest for monetary gain lends credence to the fear that international syndicates have already (or will soon) become involved in the trafficking of nuclear weapons. In some locations in Russia, where organized crime seems to have grown stronger than the government itself, the materials used to make nuclear bombs are guarded by underpaid and often disgruntled workers and stored in nothing more secure than the kind of lockers used in American high schools.

The prospect of nuclear weapons becoming readily available to terrorist groups, drug cartels, or any other illegitimate organization with enough money to spend makes it more imperative than ever to grapple with the problem of organized crime. Recently, there have been encouraging signs that the urgency of the problem has not been lost on the national governments in a position to do something about it. In 1998, strong U.S. sanctions against Colombia's "narco-democracy" encouraged Colombian voters to elect a new president who had no connections to the drug cartels. Meanwhile, the FBI, bolstered by its success in the Ivankov case, has set up legal attaché offices in 23 nations, increasing the ability of the bureau to penetrate the world of international organized crime. Also, the United Nations held a conference on international organized crime in 1994 that focused on fostering worldwide investigative cooperation and on developing common international laws pertaining to organized crime.

As it stands now, organized criminals are often able to use the many differences in the legal systems among nations to evade prosecution. The current world situation resembles the situation in the United States in the 1920s, when criminals could outrun prosecution for their crimes simply by fleeing to another state. Nations are understandably reluctant to change their own laws to match the laws of another nation. But some kind of balance must be struck on an international scale between the autonomy of each individual nation and the need for some common laws among all nations.

Senator John Kerry proposes that the United States

and its allies experiment with special courts that would enable international criminals to be tried "wherever the evidence and witnesses were located, applying the laws of the country where the crime took place." This might solve some of the perplexing jurisdictional problems associated with prosecuting today's global organized crime. "Let's imagine," Kerry writes,

> how such a system might work in a case involving a French national who has ordered a contract killing of an American in Thailand by an Italian as a result of a failed heroin deal. Today, only Thailand would be able to prosecute such a case. At best, the Italian hit man would be the only person likely to face trial; getting the Italian courts to extradite him could take years, and the likelihood of his French boss being in turn extradited would be even more remote. Under the "special court" system, the United States, whose citizen was the victim and therefore might have the greatest interest in a prosecution, could take charge of the investigation, seek to extradite the Frenchman and the Italian at the same time, and apply the murder laws of Thailand in a trial at a special court in Washington. If convicted, the Frenchman and the Italian could then either serve their sentences in the United States or be returned to serve time at home. Either way, the chances of justice being served would be substantially increased over the current situation.

If balances need to be struck in the realm of international law, they need to be struck in domestic laws as well. In the United States, one tool proven to be highly useful in the battle against organized crime has been the wiretap. But this tool, along with all other forms of government surveillance, has the potential to endanger the privacy of innocent citizens. The possibility exists that the continued legalization of ever-more-widespread government surveillance could help facilitate severe government abuses. Such abuses occurred in the past in the Soviet Union and Eastern Europe, where the ability of the government to spy on its citizens led to a near total erosion of individual freedom. In other words, tools like wiretaps should be used carefully, as if their misuse could lead to the very crumbling of democracy.

Integrity at all levels of government is among the most important factors in the fight against organized crime. This is because the flip side of governmental integrity, governmental corruption, has played a major part in the development of every significant organized crime group in history. In the 1800s, for example, crooked politicians helped build ragged street gangs into thriving neighborhood empires of crime, and in the 1920s misguided legislation and epidemic corruption elevated small-scale operations into nationwide industries. Conversely, when state and federal agencies have made integrity a priority—as was done in the 1930s with the Secret Six and their law enforcement creation, the Untouchables—organized crime has been notably weakened.

The most vital element in any organized crime operation is a demand for illegal goods or services. The Prohibition era offered ample evidence to support the belief that if a high enough demand exists for an illegal product, criminals will find ways around the laws. This dynamic has repeated itself on a global scale since the 1960s in the workings of the international narcotics industry. The U.S. government's "War on Drugs" of the 1980s and 1990s has done little to hamper the illicit industry, in large part because the demand for drugs remains high.

Awareness of this failure has prompted growing support for a shift in the focus of government policy away from viewing the drug problem as a "war" to viewing it as a problem of public health. Supporters of this shift in policy, like Mayor Kurt Schmoke of Baltimore (who branded the so-called War on Drugs a "domestic Vietnam"), want to see the bulk of available tax dollars going to effective drug education programs and addiction treatment centers rather than to quasi-military operations against international drug cartels. With this approach, Schmoke believes, the demand for drugs would decrease significantly, thus drying up large portions of the illegal narcotics industry.

Organized crime has become a sickness shared by virtually every nation in the world. The sickness calls for an international response. But, as can be seen from the damage inflicted by the illegal narcotics trade on neighborhoods, families, and individuals, it also cries out for a more local reply. Organized crime can be weakened by anyone willing to work to create communities in which there is a low or even nonexistent demand for illegal goods and services, and in which impoverished young people like the Vietnamese immigrant Tinh Ngo aren't cast out into the street like dust. Such communities hit organized crime like a bullet right between the eyes.

# Further Reading

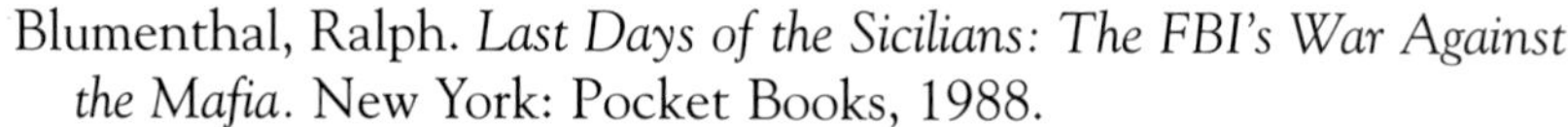

Blumenthal, Ralph. *Last Days of the Sicilians: The FBI's War Against the Mafia*. New York: Pocket Books, 1988.

English, T. J. *Born to Kill*. New York: Avon Books, 1995.

Fox, Stephen R. *Blood and Power: Organized Crime in Twentieth-Century America*. New York: William Morrow and Company, 1989.

Kelly, Robert, ed. *Organized Crime: A Global Perspective*. Totowa, N.J.: Rownan and Littlefield Publishers, 1986.

Kenney, Dennis J., and James O. Finckenauer. *Organized Crime in America*. Belmont, Calif.: Wadsworth Publishing Company, 1995.

Kerry, John. *The New War: The Web of Crime That Threatens America's Security*. New York: Simon & Schuster, 1997.

Kinkead, Gwen. *Chinatown: Portrait of a Closed Society*. New York: HarperCollins, 1992.

Kleinknecht, William. *The New Ethnic Mobs: The Changing Face of Organized Crime in America*. New York: The Free Press, 1996.

Márquez, Gabriel García. *News of a Kidnapping*. New York: Alfred A. Knopf, 1997.

Sante, Luc. *Low Life: Lures and Snares of Old New York*. New York: Farrar, Straus, Giroux, 1991.

Sifakis, Carl. *The Mafia Encyclopedia*. New York: Facts On File, 1987.

# Index

# Index

JOSH WILKER is the author of several books for young readers, including two previous books in the Chelsea House CRIME, JUSTICE, AND PUNISHMENT series, *Classic Cons and Swindles* and *Revenge and Retribution*. He lives in the Brooklyn neighborhood where Al Capone grew up.

AUSTIN SARAT is William Nelson Cromwell Professor of Jurisprudence and Political Science at Amherst College, where he also chairs the Department of Law, Jurisprudence and Social Thought. Professor Sarat is the author or editor of 23 books and numerous scholarly articles. Among his books are *Law's Violence*, *Sitting in Judgment: Sentencing the White Collar Criminal*, and *Justice and Injustice in Law and Legal Theory*. He has received many academic awards and held several prestigious fellowships. He is President of the Law & Society Association and Chair of the Working Group on Law, Culture and the Humanities. In addition, he is a nationally recognized teacher and educator whose teaching has been featured in the *New York Times*, on the *Today* show, and on National Public Radio's *Fresh Air*.

## Picture Credits

page

2-3: AP/Wide World Photos
12: Reuters/Corbis-Bettmann
17: Agence France Presse/Corbis-Bettmann
19: UPI/Corbis-Bettmann
22: Library of Congress, #LC-P401-12426
24: Library of Congress, #LC-USZ-62-22466
27: UPI/Corbis-Bettmann
30: Library of Congress, #LC-USZ-62-15182
35: AP/Wide World Photos
38: UPI/Corbis-Bettmann
40: UPI/Corbis-Bettmann
46: Daily Mirror/Corbis-Bettmann
49: AP/Wide World Photos
51: UPI/Corbis-Bettmann
54-55: AP/Wide World Photos
59: UPI/Corbis-Bettmann
61: Agence France Presse/Corbis-Bettmann
64: UPI/Corbis-Bettmann
67: Library of Congress, #LC-USZ-62-46269
69: Courtesy The United Nations
72: Reuters/Mark Cardwell/Archive Photos
74-75: Reuters/Corbis-Bettmann
77: UPI/Corbis-Bettmann
78: Agence France Presse/Corbis-Bettmann
82-83: AP/Wide World Photos
86: Reuters/Corbis-Bettmann
87: AP/Wide World Photos